more praise for

BLUE THROAT OF DAY

"*Catfish McDaris' Blue Throat of Day is a meta-experiment; a seamless Tao of poetry and prose that juxtaposes a wide array of sensibilities for you to trip. He narrates some of the most interesting batshit crazy stories, but with the calmness of a Bodhisattva. There is a strange reception of differing highs of human condition in his poems; and he narrates it with such a vigor, humor and strangely beautiful/exotic imagery. One of the most important beat voices of our generation, Catfish McDaris has pulled out another masterpiece in the shape of Blue Throat of Day, which will be remembered, thought and talked about and loved for a long.*"

— Sudeep Adhikari, PhD, Kathmandu, Nepal

"*Blue Throat Of Day by Catfish McDaris is a treasure to behold: If you are familiar with McDaris' work I can tell you that you will be far from disappointed and if this is your first look at McDaris, you will want to go on and read his other publications: The poems and short fiction pieces in this book take you on a varied and colourful journey: the style and rhythm and subject matter move effortlessly as McDaris is a weaver of words whose imagery and music is in a place of its own and this makes McDaris a unique poet, a finely tuned craftsman of his art: from the opening piece: 'Burn it the Fuck Down' through to the final poem 'Eight Rules For Defecating In Nature' there is a flow that keeps moving, elegantly and easily and it drives you forward wanting to read the next poem or story: McDaris' sense of humour wanders through this book and it can be barbed, gentle and explosive but always real and truthful: Blue Throat Of Day is a book that you'll keep returning to again and again, buy it and find out.*"

— John D Robinson, Holy&intoxicated Publications

"Catfish McDaris' engaging assemblage of gritty, sensual, working class characters thrive, or barely get by, in second-hand stores, down on the Bowery, and low rent establishment. They bring home whiskey, malt liquor and sausages in ancient autos that barely run. They often set their hopes on Lotto Games with the smoke and mirrors of life where luck is a "fickle bitch" at best. The prose is at once incisive, humorous and intimate. But it isalways serious — always life at the ragged edges. Though various lusts run throughout the collection, what McDaris writes of human nature is funny and often sadly true at the deepest levels of ourselves. Blue Throat of Day is a generous offering, an expansive, engaging collection, written in McDaris' distinctive style, essential reading for those who love poetry and prose written eloquently from the gut."

— Jeffrey Alfier, Founder and Co-editor, Blue Horse Press and San Pedro River Review

"With Blue Throat of Day, Catfish McDaris gives us a marvellous "hurricane of dreams" which level with humour, surprise with image and prove yet again why McDaris is a true innovator and master of the written word. Blue Throat follows his life in the army, years as a postie, takes us through Mexican hillsides, Buddha shopping in New York, fake moon landings and many places beyond mere geography. The characters he creates are rich with shortcomings we can believe in, root for and ultimately relate to. Fine art is a recurring theme - the lives of Frida Kahlo and Vincent Van Gogh in particular - which was a great pleasure for me as a reader. So much verve and imagination racing through each poem like maddening bits of "sunlight [that] sliced the clouds like a tomahawk." Catfish McDaris is the real deal and Blue Throat of Day will show you why."

— Ryan Quinn Flanagan, author of "The Blue of Every Flame"

BLUE THROAT OF DAY

new and selected poems

poems by

CATFISH MCDARIS

STUBBORN MULE PRESS
DEVIL'S ELBOW, MO

Stubborn Mule Press

Devil's Elbow, MO

stubbornmulepress.com

Copyright (c) Catfish McDaris, 2018
First Edition 11 7 5 3 2 1
ISBN: 978-1-946642-89-9
LCCN: 2018965485

Design, edits and layout: Jeanette Powers
stubbornmulepress@gmail.com
Cover Image: Elim J. Sidus, elimvolkaija@gmail.com
Author photo: Cynthia Diane Mancuso

contact Catfish McDaris: mcdar3@aol.com

to my small press family ...

CONTENTS

INTRODUCTION:

He tried normalcy, but love was
a delicate butterfly, in a tornado,
a facade of yearn and desire

Drink helped to forget to remember,
like ships inside bottles evading
the tedium of a burning world
                    —from "Gone Amazon"

I honestly can't remember the first time I read Catfish McDaris' work, or where I first heard of him. He's one of those poets that's been publishing and a part of the literary scene in general for so long that it's just a given that you know who he is if you read poetry at all. In fact, when I first moved to Minnesota in the mid-'90s and asked local poets who the big Midwest poets were, Catfish McDaris was almost always one of the first names to come up. Years later, when my kids were finally old enough that I could consider reaching out to other writers in my community, I began corresponding with Catfish myself.

During the course of our friendship, he's referred me to some local poets that I might not have bothered finding on my own, at least one of which has become a good friend. It's kind of a litmus test-Catfish has fabulous taste in poets, and if he takes the time to point someone out to you, chances are they're a solid, no-bullshit type of person worth getting to know. He's also the name you drop when you want other small press poets to take you seriously.

Now, while I didn't get a chance to get to know Catfish as a living human bring until well past 2010, I already knew who he was well before that. Like most poets in the small press, we'd crossed times in print dozens of times in little photocopied zines and independent literary journals over the past few decades. When I moved to Minnesota, one of my neighbors (who wrote under the ill-conceived pen name, Wolf Vest), was co-publisher at Pariah Press, which published Catfish's 1999 poetry collection, "The Wolf Pack." When that book came out, it was a really big deal in my little circle of poetry-publishing friends. But even earlier than that, I was a planning committee member of the first and second Underground Press Conference in Chicago. Catfish read at the 1993 conference, and while I didn't get to attend myself due to a severance check being lost in the mail in between moving from California to Florida, I was well familiar with his work.

Throughout his writing career, Catfish has written a staggering amount of material, published a staggering amount of material both in book and magazine form by publishers and publications around the world, and edited an co-edited a staggering number of journals and anthologies. His poetry draws heavily on images of Americana, tumbleweeds, blank vistas designed only for spectacular sunsets, and the occasional flurry of snow. The desert and wide, open spaces figure largely in these poems, while the people who live in these poems are often sex-starved, depraved, yet magnetic and immensely identifiable. While he's been a longtime Wisconsin resident, he's originally from the sunshine and wide deserts of New Mexico, and the landscape of those painted sands permeates his work like lovesick memories. I'm not going to hypothesize on this too much, but I know for myself that these long Minnesotan winters I've learned to endure make me miss the ocean to a painful point—I imagine that

Catfish must look out his windows at the thigh-high snowdrifts of January in Wisconsin and wonder what the hell he's doing trapped behind ice when there is an "alkali desert, blazing white hot from the merciless sun" at the far end of I-40. Characters make repeated appearances through this collection, dominant is that of the the story of Porterhouse, who careens through the treacherous world of wild women with a bottle of hard liquor in one hand and a pen for writing his poems in the other. There's a Spaniard that makes his appearance in several poems, too, spending his time on leave from his military post to follow poets and women.

There's a "Smoofy" and a "Reefer" and a "Puma" that show up in these poems, too, with tangled stories about their crude and beautiful dramas with friends and women. The Post Office—the torturous, economic lifeline of so many poets and writers, famously, Charles Bukowski and William Faulkner—makes its appearance here many times as well. The stories drift in an out of what could be reality and what is obvious fantasy, with blurred lines in between—in one particularly terse piece, a father has to saw a pit bull's head off to get it to stop chewing his daughter's leg off. And, holy cow, there's a lot of fucking in this book. A superficial glance at the pages of this collection would tell you that this book is either not for the prudish or squeamish in general, or that it is the perfect gift to give someone who needs to loosen the fuck up.

The big thing about Catfish's poetry is that yeah, you can say his poems are "about" things, like I just did, and give a half-assed summary of each, but any simplistic definition is thrown off by the beauty and skill in which these poems are assembled. Catfish places words together like they're pieces of a complex puzzle, putting each irregular-shaped, perfect word next to another to create a scene as stark and sharp as a Posada woodcut or a Lange photograph. You don't just read these poems—you step into them, live inside them as you read them, and come out after the last stanza wanting more.

Luckily for you, dear reader, this is a huge collection, big enough to get lost in. Take a ride out to the desert in a beat-up pick-up truck with a bottle of cheap whiskey and some decent, fun, foul-mouthed company in the seat beside you, and you might find yourself becoming a character in this book, too.

~Holly Day

BURN IT THE FUCK DOWN

Mamas crying for their sons
war is for the rich motherfuckers
to pad their bank accounts

There are no sides
no borders
no religions

It's all greed and hate
death songs on the wind
blood and tears soaking the earth

All ancient wisdom is
silent
it's all been written and read

The sky crumbles into
a sheet of fire rain
shark river where salt
water crocodiles and piranhas
live with the killers
and denizens of the deep.

RED PURSE FULL OF MARIJUANA

Kaleidoscope plumbago on a zephyr wind
jasmine, honeysuckle, and lilac perfume
wafting in the vibrating heat wave as I wait

Rivers thunder mellow jazz ravens dancing in
the banana trees, time is wiser than people,
dying is just waking up on another tomorrow

Tears of God the panther ate the rose, a delicious
morsel of ghost, memory, rain, for two months
I waited by the house in San Angel and Casa Azul

Sitting for a cafecito and churro, a red purse full
of marijuana appeared, soft hands covered my
eyes, "Do you like mota, gringo?" she asked
"When I was a hippie, I toked," "What's a hippie?"

I told her as we took a taxi to a park where they
trained bulls for the corrida. "When the matador
kills them I feel their pain, like my accident."

SPACKLING COMPOUND

Hands too damned shaky to be a pickpocket or
a poet, eating crooked duck in Chinatown,
studying the abattoir AKA bank robbery

An alligator smiled from the piano it played,
both of their teeth gleaming white, a clown
flew through the clouds, shot from a catapult

She had a hole in her heart, he was the spackling
compound, thinking each person can find
their paradise; the location, an age, a person,
their jail of love and be lucky to never lose it

Gila monsters and snow men cook beans and
go fishing, with no hole in the ice, casting
hooks into the air, catching black sparrows,
Canadian geese, pigeons, and flying squirrels.

It's Impossible to Tame a Mountain Man

Porterhouse's lady enjoyed giving orders
she was a fine lady, so he stayed mellow

There was a fat bunny in the yard, she
wanted him to give it a carrot, he said we

Shouldn't supply food to wild creatures,
nature would provide for all its animals

She yelled and screamed over and over,
throw it a damn carrot, he took a carrot

Hefted it in his hand and hurled it fast and
hard, it hit the rabbit in the eye and it died

Porterhouse skinned the rabbit and seasoned
it and put it on a mesquite fire for roasting.

BEYOND PISSED OFF

Rain sizzling on the asphalt
blue yellow sparks flying above
the street cars in the inky night

A bad azz broke into her house,
she was 92 years old, he said he
wanted some dope money and

He might slip her his meat, she
said you like meat, how about
some hog leg, she stuck her 357

Up his skinny butt and blew his
fucking brains all over her newly
painted ceiling, she said well fuck
a duck and went to call the cops.

MY HORSE STUCK OUT ITS TONGUE CATCHING SNOWFLAKES SO DID MY DOG AND I

The yellow finches and blue sparrows stood
in a purple blue bed of Siberian irises, they
sucked up nightcrawlers like Michelangelo
eating spaghetti with basil and virgin olive oil

The lead tore me open I made a last meal
I inhaled my noodles with a straw, death was
near me and my sucking chest wound, geysers
of bloody crimson spewed from my nostrils
and quivering lips, no more garlic or sardines

When he discovered pussy, he felt like Columbus,
he touched death and she spread her legs, using
red phone booths in the London fog calling Jack

We have a clown here that needs to be grabbed
by the pussy and a strange dead animal on his head
and flung into the streets and then put into a cage
assuming the greedy treachery like Ezra Pound.

MASTODON KUSH

Johnny dreamed about, one-eyed Juanita raising mastodons near the grassy hills of Clovis. He was glad his cousin Porterhouse was visiting, he wrote down ideas. Porterhouse's family were storytellers. They could whoop a yarn like pink cotton candy at the Santa Fe fair. Porterhouse was the dreamcatcher in the sun or moon light. He attempted to string words together, as poems or stories or songs. His parents drank rattlesnake venom, snorted devil's breath, and read to him about Houdini while he was a baby. Port was different. Him and Johnny went outside to try some wicked fucking weed. Johnny was listening to 5 Seconds of Summer. The weed was tight gummy buds interwoven with purple glowing Kush threads, washed down with tiswin. They looked up and saw seven raccoons in the cherry tree, lit up by a comet zinging across the champagne electric blue Van Gogh heavens. Port told Johnny about his latest adventure in the Jemez Mountains. He built a retaining wall for a medical clinic and helped a man with his foundation and fireplace. He met a Korean lady with all her fingers and her thumbs shortened by one digit. It got cold and Port told her it was a four-dog night. She got mad thinking he called her a dog. She said dogs are good eating too. The honeymoon hit the fan. He couldn't help looking at those nubby fingers. Johnny laughed his ass off. By morning Porterhouse had vanished into the antelope mirage distance.

LAUGHING COCKROACH

Sunlight sliced the clouds like a tomahawk,
people were frying eggs and bacon on the hoods
of their cars, Tilly was selling shoes, Lady Luck
was unhappy, ducking into a dive she ordered a draft

And opened her case, Tilly took out a matchbox and
out came a huge cockroach, the bartender grabbed a
flyswatter, but Tilly held him back, the cockroach started
singing, Hotel California and dancing, then he performed

A few flips and dove into a shot of rye whiskey. Tilly asked
if anybody would like to buy a pair of shoes, nobody said
anything, so she put the bug back in the matchbox, packed
her case and split, she got a few feet out the door and a man

Caught up with her, he said he'd like to buy the cockroach
for a thousand dollars. Tilly said she wanted three thousand,
they agreed, on two thousand, he counted out the money and
she gave him a matchbox with a roach, they got in their low
rider Tilly let the magic cockroach out, they both laughed hard.

POLAR BEARS ARE REAL BAD MOTHERFUCKERS

Out of the blue, Quick invited me to a concert at the North Pole. He said he'd won some free tickets with transportation included. The Reston, VA, based Molson Brewing Co. planned to send about 250 people for a four-day trip that included cruising the Arctic Sea from Resolute Bay aboard an icebreaker. The Red Hot Chili Peppers would entertain the group while aboard the icebreaker. A dude in the band named Flea raised sheer hell on bass guitar. The temperature was warm for the concert featuring Metallica, Hole, Moist, Cake, and Veruca Salt. We saw huge bears eating seals, Polar and Kodiak. The concert was in Tuktoyaktuk, a village on the Beaufort Sea. The winners along with about 400 townspeople gathered in a heated tent for the show. Quick and I partied with some funky ladies from Hole and some Eskimo babes. The stars were pulsing hypnotic blue diamonds. The wind was moaning on the tundra. Quick decided to wrestle a bear, I guess he just got tired of living. The Polar bear hit him once with his massive claws and his head went flying, the bear picked up his body and strolled away. I went over and looked at Quick's head, he was still smiling.

SANTA CLAUS ON EIGHT

Snow kept piling up like dead sheep on an iceberg,
I burned my wooden leg and teeth and started on the
furniture, next came her wooden Buddha collection

Cold wouldn't describe the agony of the weather,
I thought about the J shape of candy canes used
for the celebration of Baby Jesus' birthday

Hearing an eerie howl, the devil came down the chimney
like Santa Claus with syphilis on an eight ball of heroin, he said
he needed to shit, I told him the toilet was out of order

The water was frozen, he stuck his red ass in the sink,
his eyes bulged and he blew a smoke ring, he slapped his
dirty hairy pointed tail up against the wall trying to clean it

Turning around I saw all the candy canes on the Christmas
tree were red and Beelzebub was vanishing up the fireplace
with all our presents, I grabbed his nuts and was jerked up the
chimney like a dead canary in a coal mine, I passed out

The next day, my lady asked how come I was so black and
what happened to her Buddha's, I just shrugged and went to
light a fire with my magic matches the Allumettes Longues
Langes Lucifers, a smelly sulfuric volcano erupted.

MEXICAN STRAITJACKET

The goddamn newspaper said
the electric bill was going up
and it would cost more to flush
the toilet, Quick thought holy shit

What's next, there he was sitting
on the porcelain deposit throne
smoking a Mexican cigarette

He heard the doorbell and Poe
yelling, "Get up you lazy bum,
let's go to the cockfights"

Quick opened the door and let him
in, he said, "Man, you don't look
so hot" "No shit motherfucker, you
lined me up blind

With that chick from London,
we went to a British café and ate
some bloody lamb chops then she
ordered spotted dick for both of us

I finally got her home and we
were drinking gin and tonics,
she got drunk and broke my
sun glasses, so I got some

Super glue and was putting them
back together, she stuck her finger
in and glued a piece of glass up

her nose, I dropped her off at

The emergency room and parked
my car and an ambulance pulled in
and this crazy fucker was in a strait-
jacket, he jumped out and tried to

Fuck a fire hydrant, I decided it was
time to split."

DRUNKEN WEST MILWAUKEE BLUES

Drinking mezcal chewing up the worm
listening to Santana's Blues For Salvador
the police car shined a spotlight in my van

This Barney Fife looking motherfucker
swaggered up and asks me if I've been
drinking, I nod my head and take a swig

"Keep your hands where I can see them
and get out of your car," I finish the bottle
I get out slowly, he has his pistol pointed

At me, "That's not nice," "What did you
say?" I did my magic on him and reached
out and took his gun away, I pointed it

At his chest and said, "How does it feel?"
I gave him some gunslinger tricks, threw
it up in the air, caught it behind my back

I ejected the magazine and unchambered
the round in the barrel, faster than sight, I
put it in his holster and raised my hands.

CHEROKEE ROSE

Prolonging the heartbreak, baby
baby, your love leaves me on a
ten story ledge watching the side
walk artists below creating master-

Pieces vanishing in the rain, they
smile like hundred-dollar bills are
pouring down, they know that every
thing is temporary even blossoms

Floating on the xeric wind, apricots
and nectarines make fiery love and
replace the sun in the cinnamon sky,
watching a video of Tommy Castro

And the Painkillers, play his song,
Ride, pretty ladies dancing, while he
Kerouac struts past City Lights Books,
keeping me alive like a Cherokee Rose.

FRENCH KISS BLUES

His dad said he was going to
buy some Camels and never
came back, five years later he
sent a photo of himself on a double

Humper in front of the pyramids,
Spaniard hooked up with a chick
with a black belt, when someone
pissed him off, he sent her to kick

Ass, she was good in bed, but bitched
about his cat, Fido, he started putting
Fido's shit in her scrambled eggs, she'd
make ugly faces and Spaniard laughed

He decided to show her how much he
loved Fido, he grabbed a fresh turd and
ate it, then gave her a big sloppy French
kiss, that was almost the last straw, but

She loved Spaniard and hung tough, they
came home one night and some stinky
motherfucker was sitting on their toilet,
he got up to run, but Fido clawed him in

His bare ass, he didn't even flush, the son
of a bitch was a cat burglar, he refused to
steal Fido, Spaniard flushed away the stench,
while he watched, his woman get tough.

QUE PASA COATI

Porterhouse crossed the Rio Grande
north after months below the border,
he was sad almost demented, his primo
hung around waiting on him to open up

"I met a lady that saw a beaver get hit
by a car, she wrapped it in a blanket and
went home to get a container for it, thirty
minutes later, she returned to find a man
having sex with the now dead beaver

"I read about a fifteen-year-old in Siberia
that became so distressed about losing a
video game, he committed suicide by de-
capitating himself with a chainsaw

"I became acquainted with a senorita, we
danced all night and I slept on her mother's
couch, the sister of my friend was sent to
the street to empty the garbage, the truck
smashed and crushed her beyond recognition."

EVEN DEATH CAN MAKE A MISTAKE

Love is a huge blood diamond
shoved up the ass of a virgin Zulu

Love is an alligator's yellow tooth
worn by a gypsy mojo priestess

Love is a black baby dying of starvation

Love is a palomino stallion falling
into the Grand Canyon

Love is the workers getting overtime
wages on the Great Wall of China

There is no such thing as love.

DIPSTICK BLUES

Angelinos with tattoos made of cocaine,
you could snort right off and watch
the skin change until the next time
they wanted to be a human billboard

Having invented the Magic Straw, I was
richer than Hitler, I bought a crib in the
Pecan Mountains and became a master of
disguise, I was a chameleon of accents

I used the funky names like Fink and Dipstick
and many more unsavory handles, my cook
was missing her thumb, I wondered if I ate it,
I looked up at the blue night and played mandolin

Deciding to give my money to homeless vets,
Native Americans, and the needy, I would ask
them to buy and cremate Mount Rushmore and
turn it into a vast vegetable garden and orchard.

ANGELINA

Being new to California, Porterhouse adjusted to the sway of the Angelinos and palm trees. Surfboards, skateboards, smiles, and bikinis, what was not to like. Porterhouse's pockets were flush, he'd been breaking horses in New Mexico. He learned how from the Apaches and his father, they took them into water and learned the horse's language. When a wild animal is treated with respect, miracles often happen. Porterhouse got a room with a stove and a bathroom near the beach. The ocean was a new experience, he listened to the waves and tried to hear the fish singing. He stood on the beach and picked up a hand full of sand, smelling it slowly. It was like a desert, but full of salt water, full of many things to learn. Watching the golden buttery sunset, this seemed like a magnificent adventure. Porterhouse got thirsty and his stomach was growling. He stopped and bought two bottles of Archer Roose Carmenere Chilean wine and a corkscrew. At the market he bought green onions, flour tortillas, canned frijoles, and hamburger meat. From above he heard a whimper sob, he saw a few bloody feathers on the sidewalk. Half hidden in a tree was a winged lady. She was blonde and had a blue suit on and long white feathered wings. Except one wing was clearly injured.

"I need help, I've been hurt by a drone helicopter."

"How can I help?" Porterhouse asked.

"I have money, please rent a hotel room near a park with lots of birds. Also, I need a large trench coat to conceal my wings and a first aid kit. Will you help, please?" She dropped a large stack of hundred-dollar bills.

"Are you an angel?" She nodded yes. "Stay there and I'll be back." Porterhouse grabbed his bag, tossed his grub, got a nice big London Fog trench coat, got a first aid kit, and found a fancy hotel with room service. "Are you ready, Angel?"

"Don't drop me, cowboy." She floated down into his arms and smiled through a grimace. He helped her into her new coat and removed the tag. They passed a nice forested park on the way to their hotel. Porterhouse let her take a shower, then he doctored her wounded wing. They ordered surf and turf and ice cream sundaes. He opened a bottle of wine, but they were both soon asleep. Porterhouse slept on a couch. Angela took the bed.

Everyday Porterhouse went into the park and gathered feathers of all sorts from the wooded area. He left them in the bathroom and wasn't sure what Angela did with them. This went on for two weeks. One quiet morning Porterhouse woke up, on the dresser were two tall stacks of hundreds. A note with a lipstick print kiss goodbye and what looked like a duck call. The note read: if you ever need me, blow the angel whistle. Porterhouse packed his rucksack, leaving the whistle, and money. He figured he was the one who saddled his horse and he'd ride it alone.

PARIS

Painted hyacinth and saffron with
brushstrokes of scarlet sulfur
peacocks in a raspberry sky,
green sleeping ducks by the
cattail forest and melodic stream

Rainbow cutthroat trout leaping
for the gnat hatch, fat frogs burping,
loons and cranes on stilts hunting

Vincent thought about the dancer
at the Crazy Horse and how she'd
asked him to steal a Van Gogh,
he painted her one instead.

BLUE THROAT OF DAY

Coltrane in the Van Gogh rain,
my boss was from Texas, she
loved me being a writer, I showed
her my latest she said, "You like
Trane?" I nodded yes, "What are
your favorite songs he plays?"

"Lazy Bird and The Night Has a
Thousand Eyes" "You must have
taken beaucoup acid, back in the
day? Who's your sketch of?"

"Vincent Willem van Gogh" "Not
bad kid" we both laughed, since I
was twice her age, back to Gauguin,
he lopped off Vincent's ear with his

Sword during an argument, they
agreed to say it was self-mutilation,
to keep Gauguin out of prison, van
Gogh never recovered his rationality.

MEXICAN BLACK

I see ears in the swirling starry night.
the sky is drunk, the sun puking lemon
juice, the moon has a toothache, the lady
asked the dope fiend to come to talk to
Jesus, he stinks of absinthe and funk.

Sometimes at night I meet
myself when I was young,
I disgust myself now

What color is the wind?
What color is an orgasm?
What color is death?

There is no sea of tranquility
There's no such thing as a small miracle

Drinking Mexican coffee as black as death
Lady Gaga drives up in a dirty Mercury
they head to the Valley of Rhinoceroses

Listening to Swordfish Trombone and
Bitches Brew overlooking Mexico City.

MOANING LIKE A BORED PROSTITUTE

Her hair was chocolate mezcaline
and Southern Comfort, she read
Therese Desqueyroux by Francois
Mauriac on the train to Canon del

Cobre, I sipped Bonide for my TB
some fucker was leaving skid marks
on the sun-bleached curtains, my Pink
Panther needed lots of love and upkeep

I gave away Johnny Cash's 66 Lincoln
with suicide doors and his 70 Rolls
Royce Silver Cloud, to my neighbors
to watch my half coyote dog, Wilbur

They needed help, 7 people using one
toilet in a small house, 3 dogs, a girl
with 17 lizards and a snake, Lucky
Louie from Juarez got the brick casa.

SHE LIKED HER DRAGON GREEN 4RD

Porterhouse was on the treadmill
at the gym, a fat chick was next to
him, she was wearing headphones

Dancing, singing, and walking, once
in a while she'd stick her arms in the
air and her stubby black pits smelled
like rotten sardines and old funky

Pussy, Porterhouse made faces at his
lady she'd start trying to kick his
ass and she'd stumble on the treadmill.

You makes me dizzy ms. Izzy

At the Farmer's Market,
Porterhouse had Izzy on
a short leash. She's very
well behaved. A lady told
him dogs are not allowed
in the market. He told her
Izzy wasn't a dog, she was
from Australia, half dingo
and half Tasmanian devil.
Izzy sensed evil, she licked
the young blonde's crotch,
then took a big shit on her
foot. Izzy wasn't welcome.

A DOUBLE VAN GOGH APPARENTLY

The drug dealer answered
the door wearing a bulletproof
vest, 45 auto in one hand
38 snub nose in the other

The cop shot him 3 times
in the chest, drug man
shot the cop in the elbow

Cop shot druggie once
in the forehead, blowing
off both his ears, they
stuck to the walls

A brunette lady reporter
in a tight yellow dress
with melon knockers

Said, "Apparently only
the shot to the head worked."

WOMEN AGREE

Going to the grocery store
with my ladies, I notice a
beautiful woman gliding
majestically behind
her shopping cart

Ending up in the line
behind her, she sticks
her long lovely red polished
fingernail into her ear

Digging out a chunk of
wax, she flicks it and it
lands on my nose

I say, "Lady" and point
at the yellow glob

She says, "You're sick"

BEATNIK BLUES

The night moaning like a whore faking
love, red neon pouring whiskey on junk-
ies watching their blood ejaculate up into
a syringe, eyelids fluttering on Whitman's
finger, dance boys dance, blow your har-
monica until sunshine orange drenches
the shadows, prisons, and asylums over
flow, spewing detritus, talking rats with
yellow jaundiced eyes and bebop cats

William S. Burroughs cut off his finger
in 1939 out of love for Jack Anderson
and sent it to Arnold Gingrich at Esquire,
later he said it was an initiation for the
Crow Indian tribe, he hoped his words
would be published, Gingrich sent Bur-
roughs a note back reading, "I greet you
at the beginnings of a wonderful career,
when do I get the corpse?" William had
love for heroin, morphine, and marijuana

His work was of mystical, occult, and mag-
ical themes, William's totem animal was a
green reindeer, his life was fleeing from one
troubled place to another, he killed his second
wife, Joan in 1951 while drunk and went to
prison in Mexico City for 13 days, they had
him for culpable homicide, he fled to Morocco
where he was accused of importing opiates, he
fled to a rundown hotel in the Latin Quarter of
Paris, to meet Ginsberg, Corso, and Orlovsky

Burroughs cooked the dragon with a burnt spoon,
a step ahead of the law, snapping fingers, to the
bongo beat, chasing daydreams down the street.

99 WAYS TO SKIN A MONKEY

Clouds of grief and guilt
enslaved to nowhere a
piece of meat crawling
with flies and maggots

Cocaine strippers and
pole trippers in the canal
brothels of Amsterdam
snow lives on mountains

Rattlesnake owls shaking
feathers in the mesquite
writing the devil's obituary
woven unreality seeing

What cannot be seen
holding hands with the
ghost of the shaman wind
maybe dementia is a dream?

SLICING WARP SPACE WITH OCCAM'S RAZOR

Once upon a time people walked on the moon
they picked up some rocks they planted some
flags they drove a buggy around then came back
Conspiracy Theory: Did We Land on the Moon

The United States grew so eager to defeat the
Soviets in the intensely competitive 1960s
space race they faked all 11 Apollo missions
it was all a hoax, the evidence is countless
42 years since last man ever "moonwalked"

Air bubbles coming out of space suits in "space"
let's call it space giant underwater pool one
located in US and one in Russia use of blue
screen in NASA's "broadcast" from space.
not a SINGLE photo contains a SINGLE star

When shot from the moon Earth scale compared
to the moon is wrong in all photos moon as smaller
body should look larger there is NO REAL image
taken of planet earth all are composite images

Astronauts bounce like magic or puppets an
astronaut has his finger exposed were in space
that will produce severe frost bite the landing
was recorded from a monitor to fuzzy up images

To hide cables or other mistakes during the staged
landing NASA is a large money laundering scam
why haven' t we been back Porterhouse just
listened he had a UFO in his garage and a VW

Someday you hoaxers will do better research,
what about the phone call to Richard Nixon?

SHAKING HANDS WITH THE ONE EARED DUTCHMAN

Jocko's hands shook like a
half jerked off dog shitting
razor blades, rot gut was his
Poison, he'd spill more nectar
than reached his foul gullet, he
used a bar rag or shirttail to
sponge and squeeze his elixir
Down his parched gizzard, the
crack skeezer slouched against
him, looking for crumbs in an
empty eight ball dream
She used to have a walk that
screamed and whispered, I like
to fuck, long ago Jocko would
listen and turn into Van Gogh's ear
A douche bag freak tried to gank
his pile of change and steal his buzz,
a cue stick sang, it was like killing
flies with a sledgehammer
Jocko headed for the beach, the
woman said, good I don't want your
damn pity, he laid in the warm sand
until a mermaid took him home.

WATCHING THE SUN DIE

The lemon-yellow sun dribbled daylight juice onto the elephant colored rails. Taking out my last cigar, I watched the sun die. Reaching into my pocket I felt two quarters squirming, my guts were growling like a wolf man eating a vampire. I entered the hobo camp smelling food beckoning my quivering taste buds. I saw men with brown bags, holding strong fortified vino. Laying my money and stogie next to the campfire, a man dished me up a plate. Saluting him and smiling my thanks, I knew I'd have to find work, but for now one thing was certain, someone sure could cook. After meeting up with my Pueblo amigo, Puma and building a fireplace in Espanola, New Mexico, I felt restless. I suggested a trip to New Orleans. Puma had never seen the Mississippi and I wanted to consult with a voodoo woman, I'd heard about.

Walking down Bourbon Street, listening to Dixieland jazz and blues, once in a while we would start dancing. Musicians and tourists gawked and grinned. Puma borrowed a guitar and I sang some songs in Spanish and recited a few poems. An old man jumped off his porch and played congas, flute, and harmonica. Several coins and bills were deposited into the gent's sombrero. He fed us hot gumbo and crawdads and we drank chicory coffee laced with hooch. The house of the voodoo woman was in an alley near the river. Puma recognized most of the herbs hanging from her ceiling beams. There were jars of chicken and goat feet and eyeballs of all sizes and pungent repugnant odors. I asked for a cure for baldness, she mixed several ingredients and took it behind a curtain for a minute. When she returned, she instructed me to stir it well before drinking. Once you return home, she said use your own warmed urine. Puma was trying to keep a straight face.

When we got back to the mountains, I decided I wasn't cooking any piss and I damn sure wasn't drinking it. Puma and I drank the datura tea, near the Painted Desert. Flocks of ravens perched on azure rocks pecking slowly at purple lizards. Stag horn cholla, agave stars, and barrel cacti leaned west toward the sun and Pacific. A turtle dove nestled in the paloverde. Puma pointed at a red rattler swallowing a kangaroo mouse. Clouds exploded in crimson, green, yellow, orange, intaglio; surrealistic bleeding hallucinations. Overpowered and frightened, we drank mezcal until oblivion accepted us.

The next day we boarded a freight train south for Oaxaca and the pyramids. Near the zocalo in Mexico City, I went to buy blue agave tequila. An old woman called to me, I reached for a few pesos. As I put the coins in her hand, she held onto mine and rubbed it with red powder. Her voice took on an unearthly quality. I felt dizzy and my legs were watery. The day became dark; the sun was swallowed by evil thunderheads.

She spoke in what sounded like German. "You will live a few more years, and then die like a dog." She wanted more money, I staggered away, feeling a terrible need to be scratched behind my ears.

SWIMMING WITH THE WILD HORSES

Nine caballos in a spring fed pond
Lady Madonna blessed them all
Mick Jagger did the English rooster
on the telly with a wide-open mouth

Porterhouse started writing this poem
Sue his supervisor had just graduated
from the little Hitler school, the Post
Office required all bosses to attend

Sue's hair was Texas blonde, she wore
skintight pants, everyone called her Ms.
Camel Toe, you could plainly see her
pussy, Porterhouse just wanted to be left

Alone with his words, Sue came out of
the ladies room with a toilet seat cover
sticking out of her jeans, Porterhouse
told her secretly, she blushed bright red

She asked him if he'd help her move a
couch at her new house, they arrived
he asked where to do you want it, she
just smiled and poured them some gin

There was a nice blanket on the couch
it had three cushions and a double camel
toe between the cracks, Sue returned in a
red see through nighty, they moved the
fucking couch all night long like maniacs.

LIZ AND VAN GOGH

Francis Taylor acting on behalf of an anonymous client,
bought a Van Gogh painting, Vue de l'Asile et de la
Chapelle de St Remy the identity of his client was Elizabeth
Taylor, his daughter, her interest in the painting had been
kept secret, the Van Gogh was in Gstaad and on her yacht
Kalizma, now in Bel Air

A California court is being asked to decide whether the
painting was among Jewish-owned works of art that
disappeared during the Nazi period, from 1933 to 1945,
if a judge finds that Nazi policy towards the Jews was
responsible for the loss she will have to return it to the
original owners or their heirs, Margarete Mauthner,

A Jewish art collector living in Berlin until she and her
family were forced to flee Germany, to South Africa in
1939, where she died in1947 she was an early champion
of Van Gogh, the legal struggle between the screen legend
and the Mauthner descendants threatens to become one of
the most bitter conflicts over a work of art ever

To reach the courts, the Van Gogh would probably fetch at
least £10m both sides are adamant that it's not the money
that matters the claimants' case against Elizabeth Taylor
is based on evidence that Frau Mauthner owned the Van
Gogh until 1939, but didn't have it when she fled to South
Africa, it is possible that she sold it

Elizabeth Taylor does not accept that the Van Gogh falls
into the definition of an artwork lost to its owner as a result
of Nazi policies, lawyers state that the claimants have no

evidence that the painting ever fell into Nazi hands, Taylor goes further, suggesting that Mauthner sold the painting to finance their escape to an art dealer before

The Nazis became the German government in 1933, Elizabeth Taylor's lawyers argue that the Mauthner heirs should be barred from bringing Solomonic wisdom, since she's owned the painting for 40 years, in the meantime, Dame Elizabeth Taylor wonders for how many years more she'll be able to admire the View of the Asylum and Chapel of St Remy

AMERIKA

Nobody is warm, everyone is hungry,
the road can eat you alive, it's not all
hobo heaven, Jack Kerouac dreams, bar
room Bukowski's telling jokes for drinks

Houses of cardboard around the fire,
growling bellies lining up waiting on
beans and tortillas, dreams of pretty
ladies, rotgut in dark smoky taverns

A cherry in your whiskey, an olive in
your gin, slow your roll or your dead
before you begin, another dog without
a day or a bottle of ice cold beer.

WINTER FOOD

The autumn days were warm, but the smell of snow was in the air. Winter was coming soon to the high country. Blue Horse, Black Knife, and Wolf Cloud were hunting on the western slopes of the mountains. The forest where they hunted was pine, fir, juniper, yew, blue spruce, and the white barked aspen. Blue Horse had taken mink, weasels, and silver and red fox in traps for their fur for his wife, Laughing Moon.

To the east was an alkali desert, blazing white hot from the merciless sun, where their enemies lived. The three warriors used spears, bow and arrows, throwing sticks, and slings to provide them with food. They prayed over each animal, thanking their departed spirits. Everything was sacred to them, animals, plants, water, fish, the earth, and the love of family. While war was always waged, one must respect and pray for enemies and a clean death.

The game was plentiful and they were having good luck. Mule and white tail deer, elk, and turkeys had been smoked and seasoned with chile piquin, a chile favored by birds. They built their smoking fires from dried wood and under trees with big branches to dissipate the smoke. The meat was wrapped in skins and tied in bundles onto pack horses for travel. An antelope had been killed on the lower slopes, but they found the meat too lean and stringy, they ate it, but wanted meat with a bit more fat.

Bears were foraging elderberries and dewberries, getting ready for winter hibernation. The men were giving bears a wide berth. Suddenly a grizzly with a scarred nose stood on its hind legs and sniffed the air. Catching the scent of men it must have remembered the wound it still carried. It roared out of the brush swinging its vicious claws. Wolf Cloud buried a spear in its throat, that didn't faze the bear. Blue Horse let an arrow fly with a second arrow following it a split second later.

The giant grizzly fell like a tree hit by lightning. The warriors gathered around with knives drawn in case the bear had more fight left in it. Both arrows entered the bear's left eye piercing its brain.

SUBJECTED TO THE LAWS OF GRAVITY AND FRICTION

All he wanted was to fly,
birds, butterflies, mosquitoes,
helicopters, airplanes, bullets,
and ladybugs all could do it

He attached wings to his body,
flapped his arms and jumped
into the air, all to no avail

Becoming angry with earth, he
bore a hole in the ground and
inserted his penis and started
fucking crazily like a sex maniac

The cops came and dragged him
away, beating his bare ass with
a baton, asphalt burning his face

They threw him in a cage,
where he never flew, but
he did learn to pull a train.

DEFACING THE MAIL

The post office let all the clerks be mail carriers for one day. My assignment was to drive around and empty all the deposit boxes in a certain section of the city. So, I followed my map and went from box to box and emptied all the letters and small packages into the back of the blue jeep. It was mundane, but it got me out of the building for a change.

I'm driving along, and I see a shapely brunette walking a small dog. She waves me down and asks for a ride. I know this is against regulations, but I like her pink toenails. "Hop in babe," I tell her. She has her dog on her lap, her blue dress starts scooting up her long legs. I soon figure out she has no panties on. I grab the dog and toss it in back, so I can get a better view. Looking in back the dog is pissing all over the mail.

"Do you want to bury your bone?" she asks, as she plays with herself. I pull over on a shady stretch of pavement. She's got her tits out and dress up and yanks my pants around my ankles. The dog takes a shit on somebody's birthday card. I get it in and start really working and this giant rat jumps out of nowhere and grabs the dog by the throat. The dog is getting murdered and the woman is screaming, and this just turns me on more. I'm trying to bust both nuts into heaven. The woman and what's left of the dog jump out of the jeep, half naked and attempts to beat on the rat. The rat jumps back in the jeep, landing on my dick, clawing and chewing and I erupt all over everything.

The woman starts running down the street but drops the dog. I try to chase her down, but end up running over the dog, killing it. I gather up the dog waffle and later throw it in a mailbox I had emptied before. The woman is a ghost. I figure, I've fucked a beauty, got blown by a rat, made breakfast out of a dog and mailed it. In the process I committed, the number one postal sin, defacing the mail. I drove back to the post office.

The dock boss asked me how my day was.

"It was kind of boring, but not too bad."

FRIDA'S GOLD

The color of rage, anger, love, hemorrhaging of the sun
on the ox gore face, velvet cocoon eyebrows ready to
fly away, you can live your life in a birdcage or soar
over oceans, mountains, jungles, swamps, and deserts

The bus and trolley accident broke Frida's spinal column,
collarbone, ribs and pelvis, fractured her right leg in 11
places, and dislocated her shoulder. Frida had polio and
one leg was shorter and the bone thinner than the other

She underwent 35 operations because of the accident,
Arias her boyfriend was with her in the crash, he
described the bus as "bursting into a thousand pieces,"
with a metal handrail ripping through Kahlo's torso,
many were injured, two died

Something strange had happened. Frida was totally nude.
The collision had unfastened her clothes. Someone in the
bus, probably a house painter, had been carrying a packet
of powdered gold. This package broke, and the gold fell
all over the bleeding

Body of Frida, when people saw her, they cried, 'La
bailarina, la bailarina!' With the gold on her red, bloody
body, they thought she was a dancer, Kahlo's path to
painting began with the collision, the greedy are selfish
fools choking on a gluttony for gold.

MESCALINE FIREFLIES

Vanilla mezcal in the indigo sky
fireflies make love and war high

Frida cut off her long ebony hair
and threw the tendrils to the wind

Diego wept blood seeing his lady in
a man's suit a monkey on her shoulder

The hair took root and grew as peyote
cacti orange and lime trees figs grapes

The wind stole the hair and spread it all
over the world Mexican wisdom paint

A wounded deer punctured by arrows at
Casa Azul her heaven she will never die.

NYC VACATION

After eating spaghetti and sausage in Little Italy, on the edge of Chinatown, my lady wanted to shop. I waited outside while she looked at Buddha's for her collection.

I watched the Bowery scene, the old brick architecture and the languages garbled together like chicken bones clogging up a garbage disposal. In a shop window I saw squirming eels, green yellow frogs, and sardines in soy sauce, next to a television displaying someone getting a foot massage and acupuncture. My toes started feeling like caterpillars frying in olive oil.

A huge fat Italian moke with a turd looking cigar stuck in his pie hole hogged up the sidewalk with his big bushy tailed red assholed dog. He trudged and stomped like he was King motherfucking Kong, looking for a challenge. A lithe little Chinaman, Bruce Lee type with a tiny brown nondescript dog tried to avoid any action, to no avail. The fight was on. The chink dog grabbed the wop dog by the nuts and did some dog Kung Fu. It was thing of beauty, blood and fur flying high.

I saw lots of gleaming meat cleavers and long knives coming out. I called my woman and said, *let's scram*.

She asked, *what have you done now.*

I just laughed.

DRINKING WITH A TALKING BOOGER

The little green man climbed
out of the can and said, "You
are a dumb drunk motherfucker
if you can see me,"

I shrugged and laughed, "Do
you think you can escape by drinking horse piss?"
I nodded and chugged a can,

"You're a sack of shit with
no guts," I opened a fresh beer

He jumped up on the can and
unzipped and pissed in the
opening with his tiny green
slimy stinking pecker

With my machete, I gave him
a split personality, drank nine
more and blew my nose, I
wrapped him with snot and
gave them a flush funeral
A pile of mail awaited, a Nobel
Prize notification, my acceptance
from the Jehovah's Witnesses,
man of the year from Alcoholics
Anonymous, acceptance into Mensa,
my Doctorate degree from Harvard,
an invitation to the White House,
nothing of interest.

THE SHOPLIFTER

Sometimes you feel like you've
entered the Twilight Zone, I was
in this supermarket and I saw a
stone fox in the condiment aisle

She opened a bottle of catsup
and chugged it down, then moved
down to the pickles and raised her
brown leather skirt and pulled her

Panties to one side and started
shoving gherkins up her vagina,
she was moaning and groaning

Then she turned and looked at me
and said, "I bet you think I'm a sour
puss" I left my basket and ran like
the bulls of Pamplona.

WRITER, PAINTER, THIEF, KILLER

I love mama poems, no Dada
poem for mama in heaven
best poem for mama
mama poems birthday
my mama poems
mama poetry in blood
poems on mama in Hindi
dear mama poem
mama naked poem

Chasing broncos, ghosts, and ladies through the night

A guy ticks off his mama, she beats him in the head with
a toaster then puts his penis in, plugs it in and clicks
it down to bagel setting.

POOR BOOGER

My uncle gave me a farm cat,
he was pretty cool mostly, but
would scratch up the furniture
and meow loud at night

I named him Booger, he always
did his business outside, slept
with me, he'd drag in a dead
bird or mouse making mama mad

Then Booger gave me the fleas,
I came home from school itching,
Booger wasn't around anywhere

I asked mama where Booger was,
she said he went to live with your
grandparents in the nursing home,
I got bad feeling about that.

IF THE MOON HAD A PUSSY I'D FUCK IT DOGGIE STYLE

Why do scumbags
always seem to
break into your
house while you're
reading Bukowski
and trying to shit?

I'd written a poem
about Uncle Willy
trying to sodomize
me and I killed him

With the back of the
toilet. His eyeballs
rolled back into his
skull and resembled
hard boiled eggs.

What a shitty way to
go, motherfucker, he
should've picked
another house, when

I hit him he squawked
like a parrot in the dark
jungle that hadn't
learned to speak human.

CAPE VALENTINE

Love is a runaway train
An elephant stampede
The Grand Canyon at sunrise
Van Gogh's bedroom
Good days bad sad dogs cats babies death
Beautiful intelligent enchanting intriguing
A memory of a memory
Back to back against the wall and the wolf
and the tax man and the ripper and the vultures
Mona Lisa's whisper and laughter
A hurricane of dreams on the precipice of life.

SHE LOVED ME BECAUSE OF POETRY

I am wood, you are fire

I am the beach, you are the ocean
when you're in my arms, nothing is wrong

I'm lying on magic clouds, waiting for you
my love is clinging to the cliff by its fingernails

"My dog ate seven cockroaches,
do you think it will get sick?"

"Naw, I used to eat them squirming
bastards swimming in hot sauce
on tortillas down in Mexico, my cholo
would do the mezcalito sombrero dance"

Six mailboxes, a coyote and a ninja
with three eyes, Hercules, Copernicus
the fear of God and love of Lucifer
dynamite stew and a brass knuckle sandwich

A saber tooth tiger and nine ants
wearing red sneakers and an
electrified rooster monkey

Some search broken dreams and
empty bottles in vain for a past
path of bloody shadows and souls

Lonely phones ring, scream and beg
while sad blue poets have visions of terror
and insatiable ravenous tigers pacing the cage

Francisco Goya's Saturn Devouring His Son
and the Man Eating Mares of Diomedes, she made
her imitation Mona Lisa smile, threw back her
long dark hair and vanished into smoke.

PAYBACK IS A FIGMENT

Her gris-gris bag was leaking
tears of blood, snitch bitches
get stitches, she wouldn't listen

Dead fish flopping on the ice
waiting on a kangaroo to save
its life and kick it in the water

Dancing blindfolded with the
devil in a mist of mystique,
kissing his hot red lips searching
for a precarious redemption

Look inside me, see my heart it
beats with pure love, but every
morning there is a filthy buzzard
salivating on my bedpost

Dreaming about Buddha on his
motor scooter, he sucker punched
me when I wasn't looking knocked
me on my ass and I had no shooter.

BEATNIKS, HOTDOGS, APPLE PIE, AND CHEVROLET

There's not a whole lot to do about death but die, her
nymphomania turned Spaniard into a kleptomaniac, the
little black dog in red panties howled at the blue moon

Spaniard heard Ginsberg went to Colorado, Micheline
was playing with Skinny Dynamite, Burroughs was
eating lunch nude and practicing his aim, he killed his
woman in Mexico City and only did thirteen days in jail

Kerouac got so pickled he swallowed himself and ended
in a giant whiskey bottle, Bukowski was at the track
checking the nags and ladies, Snyder left for the Far East

Ferlinghetti was eating Coney Island hotdogs, Ed Sanders
was Fugging around playing a musical tie, Janine Pommy
Vega was tracking a serpent, Ray Bremser sold his hat

Wanda Coleman made the voodoo angels fly, Charles
Plymell heard the buffalo cry, the tiny white dog in a
tuxedo
shimmering with diamonds and sapphires lit a blunt.

EAGLE KILLER

I made a bald eagle die
once after McDonald's,
I was in a glass
elevator in Chicago

My wife and daughter
were with me and they
almost passed out

Well dressed women
got on the elevator,
screamed and sprayed

Perfume, that pissed me
off, so I tried to fart every
three floors, when we got

To Michigan Avenue the
elevator opened and an eagle
happened to be flying over-

Head, it plummeted to the
ground temporarily stunned,
the women trampled it to death.

THE BOOGIE MAN

Spaniard would've never
thought of Boogs, but he
went to see the Rabid
Aardvarks at the bingo

Casino picking and grinning,
Boogs, was a big gross spastic
slob Spaniard worked with
at the Post Office sorting

Packages, five people would
stand at a short conveyor belt
throwing parcels into large #
two bags ready for mail carriers

Boogs had seniority so he chose
to work with women, a game of
zip code poker would begin to
break the monotony, Boogs was

Lucky, getting four nine's often,
he got his name from tunneling
up his nostrils for boogers and
wiping them on people's mail

Postal Inspectors wearing gloves
came and put him in bracelets, the
charge was defacing the mail, he
was gone and missed by no one.

MAKE YOUR MOVE

Spaniard's teeth were once razor sharp,
his muscles were hard, vision far seeing
he believed the only guarantee in life was
that one day it will end, he played chess

With his minutes, waiting to see what
he was waiting for, he refused to shit in
McDonald's, his women gave him chocolate
covered nuts, ladies with a thousand hearts

Of stone, they danced the hoochie coochie
under the harvest moon, they made their own
music, laughed in darkness and let all the
tomorrows worry about their own damn selves.

CURING BUCKET BOY

Bucket boy was the nickname Spaniard
gave Betty's son, the puking boy could
not get in a car without getting sick, so
Spaniard got him a bucket to use, within

Two blocks this kid was doing Exorcist
like vomiting, they took him to the doctor,
they found nothing wrong, so Betty let
Spaniard take him to a witchdoctor in

Hell's Kitchen, the mojo man crushed
turquoise and coral and painted his face
red and green, then he mixed some urine
and herbs and made Bucket boy swallow

It and three miniature cars, the kid looked
like death and oatmeal, the witch man
sang about rattlesnakes in Mexico City,
the boy slept and woke up all cured.

THE LUNATIC

Spaniard stopped by the Super Bar on the way home, he drank enough cheap brandy and draft beer to knock down a mule or two. Then he walked to a bookstore looking for something to help him escape. He always went to the poetry section first, to see if they had any books by him. Some tall skinny guy was bent over showing his ass crack looking at bottom shelf books. When he stood upright and farted, Spaniard felt like burying his steel toed boot up the dude's ass. When the dude bent over he farted again, Spaniard elbowed him in the kidneys. What was worse than his fart stench was his sweat, urine, dog shit slimed shoes, and he reeked like an old douche bag. Spaniard wished his sense of smell was worse than his sense of humor.

"Hey motherfucker, you should clean up your act." Smelly boy looked like he'd been hit in the head with a twenty-pound sledge hammer. He stopped and spoke with the clerks and they all looked at Spaniard. He just smiled and gave them all a little wave. After finding one book by Chekov, he went home.

Spaniard was trying to catch forty winks, it sounded like his lady, Lupe and their cat were wrestling or having sex at the foot end of the bed.

"Hey, I'm trying to sleep. The damn machine noise from the post office letter sorter is ricocheting inside my screaming skull."

The cat meowed like a Husqvarna mower was chewing and gnawing him into pieces. He thought Lupe was committing murder and mayhem. "Hold still, you little son of a bitch," she said.

"What in the hell are you doing woman?" Spaniard asked.

"I'm trying to clean the cat's ass. He took a nasty dump in the litter box and now wants to rub his ass all over my white down comforter."

"Just quit corn holing that cat, please. The fucking zip code madness won't leave me alone tonight."

"Why do you act like your hero, Bukowski?"

He screamed, "Bukowski can kiss my brown ass."

Spaniard started snoring like a constipated chainsaw sawing through an anvil.

THANKSGIVING CAN BE A REAL MOTHERFUCKER

My lady was withdrawing
$60 from the drive-up ATM
I was tuning in Steely Dan

A Nixon masked person
with a revved chainsaw
cut off her extended arm
and grabbed it and the money

Ripping my belt from my
trousers, I made a tourniquet
next thing I knew I was on
the floor in a store

A circle of frozen turkeys
were shooting dice with tiny
hands, several had cigars
puffing from their neck hole

They were cursing in Turkish,
sounding pissed off and flipping
each other the bird, looking
around I noticed I was naked

I had a cell phone, I dialed 911
the operator asked, "What is
your emergency?" all I said
was gobble gobble gobble

Waking in a pool of sweat
I saw a full bottle of 101

proof whiskey, reaching

To scratch my testicles
I trotted for the bathroom
to discover two tiny plucked
butter balls, I thought this
is worse than Naked Lunch.

THE GHOST OF LIBBY

Dreaming of Libby
Casper from the ninth grade,
she was red haired
with creamy skin and freckles

Libby must've watched
a Gypsy Rose Lee movie
she knew how to bump
and grind to the music

Her parents had a monstrous
aquarium full of goldfish,
after we had a hot make out session,

Libby told me she'd do a striptease
and remove an item of clothing
every time I swallowed a goldfish,

I used a tiny net and tried to capture
the littlest fish, they weren't bad
to swallow being all slick, they went
right down, a few started squirming
in my mouth and I spit them out and
this got Libby excited

Her pancake sized boobs
were topped with nice strawberries
when she got down to her panties,

I thought our game was over,
but she said if I ate a big goldfish

and chewed it up, she'd go all
the way, too bad her parents

Showed up just as I was blowing
remnants of fish all over their clean
shag carpet, I lit out of there like
Quicksilver on roller skates being
shot at by a bazooka.

LITTLE VIETNAM, TIGERLAND FORT POLK, LOUISIANA

"See that boot?" the drill sergeant bellowed.

"Yes, sir."

"I'm not a fucking officer, never call me sir."

"Yes, drill sergeant."

"Give me twenty push-ups and kiss the tip of my boot twenty times."

I could see my sweating reflection in his spit shined boots. Many alternatives briefly crossed my mind. Then I dropped and followed orders.

The drill sergeant wore a Smokey the Bear hat and was puffing on a stinky-assed stogie. He was a muscled throwback to the caveman days. I thought about shoving a grenade up his ass.

"Wipe the black off your lips. You look like you've been sucking on something rotten. Then report to the gas chamber." A nasty grin split his coal black face, his teeth were rat shit yellow.

The gas chamber was an old barracks with two horse troughs in front. You wore a full field pack, carried your weapon, and wore your steel helmet and gas mask. Two drill instructors made you run around the room until you were breathing hard, then they opened four canisters of mace and pepper gas. The room turned foggy and ate at any exposed skin like acid. They ordered us to halt, remove our helmets and hold them between our knees, remove our gas masks and replace our helmets on our heads.

The gas chewed at our eyes, nose, and mouth like a horde of stinging wasps on fire. The masked instructors smiled and slowly asked our name, rank, and where we were from. By this time most of us were foaming in froth like rabid dogs. We crawled outside to wash in the horse troughs, they were filled with piss and vomit.

One soldier dropped his helmet, he was ordered to return to the gas chamber the next day. That night he hung himself in the latrine. Tigerland at Fort Polk, Louisiana was the closest thing to hell and Vietnam there was in America.

In July 1971, I celebrated my eighteenth birthday there, by digging a hole with my entrenching tool, my hands bled through blisters. Mosquitoes, chiggers, ticks, and deer flies swarmed and swam in your sweat and tried to burrow into your eyes and every orifice.

"I killed three men, with that little shovel, caved their skulls into hamburger," the drill sergeant bragged. We'd just eaten greasy canned meat, chunks of squash, and lumpy potatoes for lunch.

"What's wrong, boy? You usually got something stupid to say."

"It's my birthday and I was wondering how it feels to die," I replied.

"I'll tell you when it's your birthday, you are my child now.

I am your mama, papa, and God. And if you want to know how it feels to die, I have three more weeks to teach you. Now, dig me a hole, you piece of shit."

"Yes, drill sergeant."

The concrete floors in the barracks were dyed red, so every item of white clothing soon ended up pink. Every pore of my body seemed to ooze Louisiana pink.

We went to the hand grenade pits the next day. We received a two-hour lecture and demonstration on how to pull the pin and throw it. It's destructive force and five seconds before it would explode and blow the hell out of anything around. We had a three-foot-high cement wall to hide behind after throwing the grenade. There were three pits, divided by walls. Each had a hole in the corner in case someone just dropped it. A drill instructor was supposed to kick the live grenade down the hole, in case of accident.

This duty was for instructors that had pissed someone higher up off.

Two southern boys were chosen to throw grenades at the same time as me. The first grenade toss went okay, but gravel pelted us from the sky. The drill instructor grinned. The second toss, the guy next to me couldn't get the pin out. The instructor went to help. They got the pin out, but juggled the grenade, just as the instructor kicked it toward the hole, it went off. His foot was gone, it looked like night crawlers spurting blood from his ankle. The southern boy was holding his ears, blood was pumping from his mouth and nose. His screams turned into red bubble gurgles.

Learning to kill was a bitch.

On completion of our seventh week of training, with one week to go, we were given three-day passes. A Texan, an Arizonian, and a New Mexican (me) headed for New Orleans; head shaved G.I. Joe specials.

We hit Bourbon Street and whored and drank and smoked weed. Fuck the army! We "borrowed" a car and cruised with some young nightingales and wound up in jail. The army came and got us, we were their property. We watched from a latrine window, which we were cleaning with toothbrushes, as all the other soldiers marched in the graduation parade. They were all decked out in dress green uniform and shiny.

We were recycled, eight weeks all over again, same old shit different day. All the Basic Training (boot camp) graduates got orders for specialized Army Individual Training and then were shipped onto Vietnam. We peeled potatoes, dug holes, got gassed, tossed grenades, and got inspected like cattle daily. By the time we graduated, Nixon had decided to send no more fresh American meat to Nam. They say every cloud has a silver lining, well sometimes even fucking up does too.

ALMOST

After visiting the gargoyles
of Montmartre, my lady
decided to shop

I stood outside smoking
a Gitane watching people,
a man approached and asked
if I wanted to screw his sister

I looked around, but saw no
sister, I replied no, he replied
how about my brother, he's
young and tight, I shook my head

Do you have a dog, I asked
the Frenchie looked appalled
fucking Americans, he said
walking away swiftly

My lady exited the shop,
she said did you make a
new friend, I said almost
dear almost.

TWO ZILLION WAYS

In boot camp the army
gave me a bad haircut,
it was so bad I needed a
dentist and a psychiatrist

My hair was gone, my mind
was a spewing fire hydrant,
a pocket full of ravens
whistling in the graveyard

Mountains in the fog,
buzzards on the steeple
living the nightmare of a
toothache broken dream

A rock in one shoe,
a bullet in the other,
never owned a diamond
and none have owned me

Two zillion ways to die,
in a funky junky world,
horses in a snow storm
trapped by mirror ghosts

Shape shifters chasing
vampires into Spaniards and,
Russian tumbleweeds,
trouble and bad luck

Sharks eating lions in
the Sea of Cortez,

spanking a guitar like
a naked nasty lady

A chicken fried monkey
of biblical proportions,
cranes sailing above the
Danube on a Siberian wind

Stealing minds and money
in the name of the Lord.

MEXICO CITY

The sun is the blanket
of the poor, corn tortillas
y frijoles fill the stomachs

Kerouac's Blues took a
detour, Burroughs shot his
woman and got away clean

Diego's murals bleed
sacrificed Aztec virgins,
Trotsky bludgeoned to
death with an ice axe

Frida, a wounded deer
smokes mota for pain and
paints la obra maestras

The Spanish inquisition
plays stretch with the
ghost of Montezuma

An eagle soars with a snake
in its talons above the graves
of Zapata, Juarez, and Villa

Living in the sinking paradise
of Mexico City is sometimes
like being staked to an anthill,
but always forever a nirvana.

LEFTY

I was watering the apple tree and these ants parachuted onto my arm and started biting the shit out of me. I slapped them, but for everyone I crushed, two more ants replaced them. My arm started swelling up like a fire hydrant. They spoke to each other in ant language and said, "This is the motherfucker that burned us with a magnifying glass when he was a kid, quite the serial killer. Let's bite his goddamn arm off." Those were some mean ass ants with long memories.

Now I'm known as Lefty.

THE FOUR MOONS OF JUPITER

Poe was always between
rocks and hard places, he did
not take an ounce of grief or
tribulation or annoyance

Having him for an amigo could
be dangerous and exciting, super
gorgeous women swarmed him
Poe convinced me he had

telepathic powers over birds,
he was once peeing and he made
a woodpecker land on his

He talked me into sticking my peter
in a toaster, swearing I'd be unharmed,
it damned near killed me, I thought my father
would finish the job when he quit laughing

Sometimes I miss Poe kind of like
Io, Europa, Ganymede, and Callisto.

THE PRINCE OF SAN QUENTIN

The Boogeymen were white
dudes with Afro wigs laying
down the funky hip hop

Poon was lined up as far
as the eye could see, be
bopping and rubber necking

Just waiting and hoping to
give it up to the players, I
watched the young clams
ready to catch some snatch

Sure enough I found three,
one had a purse of Peruvian
rock, another had a nickel
plated 45 and a roll of hundreds

The third had Columbian red
bud and her skin was ivory snow,
like a baby elephant's tusks

They were aching for it, we
jumped in my short and headed
to their crib

Perfumed lace panties went
flying as they all did a mean
bumping burlesque striptease

I was harder than the bars in

San Quentin, a hell hole I
liked to disremember

After taking care of biz with
my steel, I helped myself to
the other booty, the rest I'll
leave up to your imagination
and of course, mine.

A GIRAFFE SANDWICH

A curse hung in my ear, I got
the bottle, poured myself a
drink, and lit a cigarette

Whiskey calmed my nerves, I
was half asleep, I dreamed about
giant catfish in the river

My mother told me some were
so big alligators left them alone,
I caught one, its head was the
size of a man's torso, I shouted

Mother must not have heard, the
catfish kept trying to dive, I finally
let it go, I awoke like a hungry
dragon eating a giraffe sandwich.

MASTER OF THE UNDERSTATEMENT

Spaniard looked in the mirror
his eyes were full of lies

I'd rather be a testicle than a rainbow
I'd rather be a tornado than a stinky fart
I'd rather be a cherry tree than a vagina

I'd rather be Wolfgang Amadeus Mozart than Frank Sinatra
I'd rather be a buffalo nickel than a burning American flag
I'd rather be a teardrop than a booger

I'd rather be a guitar than a sneeze
I'd rather be a cloud than a flounder
I'd rather be a thimble of love than a ton of gold

I'd rather be tiger shit in Vietnam than a man with an ugly
penis
I'd rather be a clitoris than a tomato
I'd rather be William S. Burroughs' amputated finger
than Adolf Hitler's testicle he lost in World War One.

THE SKY WAS LARGER THAN AUSTRALIA AND AFRICA HAVING MAD SEX

After the 1902 sardine shortage, Quick knew he could no longer make a living fishing, so he sold his boat and fish canning factory. He drifted west and started painting. At first he stuck with landscapes, birds, and experiments, before he went on to draw and paint people.

When he got to the Pacific Ocean, there seemed to be pink marijuana clouds above Malibu. The salt air made him long for his old life, it was simple and clean. Over Tanqueray martinis, Quick watched the Angelinos, they danced as they walked, smooth and cool. He met a beautiful senorita, named Juanita, her body seemed eager, but peril lurked deep in her brown eyes. Quick drew her with a look of wanton pleasure on her face. From his sketch, he made a beautiful painting and showed it to her. Juanita was mad and embarrassed at first, but the painting was so erotic and flattering it aroused her.

He persuaded her to move in with him. Their apartment was made with adobe blocks and had viga post roof beams. It was soon filled with smoky chipotles, cilantro, tortillas, and delicious Mexican cooking aromas. She posed for him, at first clothed, then nude. They seduced each other as if every day was their last. They made galaxy shattering love knocking paintings off the walls, tipping over vases of Alcatraz flowers, scaring alley cats. Lightning and whirlwinds seemed to fill their adobe house.

Capturing Juanita like a tiger gone mad, at the height of orgasmic desire, was what he finally succeeded at. He kept a fish hook and line is his pocket for luck and so he knew they would never go hungry. Quick dreamed often of a French stockbroker that quit his life and went to Tahiti, but he'd found his home it was in the eyes of Juanita.

SKINNY DOGS AND SPOTTED HORSES

Quick traded a Bowie knife and an Arkansas toothpick for a cayuse with brown clouds across its white rump. The horse looked strong and knew how to dance and fly. Quick harnessed a rope bridle and threw an old Mexican saddle blanket over her. The horse galloped so fast, he thought his skin was peeling back like a shedding snake.

Quick rode back to the stable for his gear and the skinny black dog that he'd been giving scraps to, followed them out of town. The first night they camped under some cottonwood trees, he had some grain and there was scrub grass for the horse. He stirred up a pot of coffee and made some venison stew, throwing the dog some deer jerky.

The stars were happy and making love in the sky. Then the dog started farting and the horse must've felt challenged. The: who stepped on the bullfrog contest, was on. Quick moved his bedroll back from the fire, he didn't feel like getting all his hair singed off in case of explosion.

HOW I PULLED THE RABBIT OUT OF THE HAT

Paco's father was the finest jeweler in Santa Fe, he passed down his skill. Paco could make anything. He preferred silver, turquoise, coral, and bear claws, but would sometimes work with gold and precious gems. Paco's thirst was unquenchable, he'd drink anything at anytime, anywhere.

How he became a boss on a surveying crew for the Santa Fe National Forest Service was unfathomable to me. He spoke mostly Spanglish and was out of shape because of his constant drinking. Surveying timber roads up mountainsides isn't for sissies. Paco would sweat rivers of eighty proof and pour more booze down his throat at every stop.

One Friday night he asked if I was going to Albuquerque. I replied yes. He asked me to sell some jewelry for him. I thought about it, I'd made one successful selling trip to Milwaukee, so I agreed. He loaded up a jewelry case and put in a snub nose pistol in case of trouble. I drove south the seventy miles, past the penitentiary, across the Pueblo land of red hills, yuccas, and tumble weeds.

Old Town was packed with tourists, the plaza swarming. I gave a Navajo elder fifty bucks to share a corner of his blanket. I was hotter than a July jalapeno, doing almost four grand in business by early afternoon. I never noticed three pachucos giving me the eye. At dusk I made for the cantina overlooking the trickling Rio Grande. After a good meal of enchiladas and sopapillas washed down with several ice cold Tecates with lime and coarse salt, I felt great. I saw a phone booth in the parking lot and decided to share my good news with Paco.

"Hey amigo, I kicked ass and took names today. Seven grand and I still have a third of the merchandise." I heard a tapping on the glass behind me. "Hold on a minute, Paco." I turned around and saw three pistols and a sawed off shotgun all aimed at my chest by four greasy looking low riders. The leader had buck teeth and a steel marble eyeball. "Holy hell, Paco, I'm being robbed."

"Robbed? Robbed? That's my stuff, you gringo weasel. You're making theese sheet up," he yelled, cursing me in Spanglish. The phone booth door opened, I was facing four cases of lead poison.

"Give us your money and trinkets and we might let you live." I could hear Paco screaming in the background, "They're bluffing, don give theem jacksheet." Handing over the goods, the hoods drove off. Paco was still screaming as I hung up. That night I crashed at a friend's. At noon the next day I drove to Paco's, his wife, Ramona answered the door. "Were you really robbed?" she asked. I nodded. "Paco is pissed." I nodded again.
"You were supposed to go to Rabbit Mountain this morning. They waited as long as they could."

"Maybe we can get through by radio relay from the ranger's station?"

Thirty minutes later, Paco is cursing me and my ancestors. "You cost me ten grand and now you're probably screwing my wife."

"I'm on my way." When I arrived he was pacing the forest service cabin, a bottle of tequila almost empty. "You lying piece of crap," he bellowed grabbing my shirt. I kneed his nuts, he puked for a while. Some guys helped me clean him up and stick him in his bunk. The next morning I woke up and was staring into his blood red eyes. "You got any money?" he asked.

"Nope," I replied. I had four c-notes stashed in my boot. "Then you are going to be my gringo slave. Remember that fireplace we talked about? That's just for starters. I want a circular bull's eye window over my front door and an arch going into the backyard, all made out of iron pyrite. We can haul that fool's gold out of the old silver mines in Tijeras Canyon." I thought fool's gold, how appropriate. "Every waking hour we're not surveying or fighting fire, you belong to me."

I used all my talents with a trowel that my family taught me. We heaved the stones into a bucket and winch set up over a four month period, I completed all the work. I had never worked so hard or been that long without a woman. Ramona was a big woman, Rubenesque and intelligent. She could really rustle up the grub and had an inviting smile.

Paco didn't appreciate what he had. He'd bring his drunken amigos over to show them his white slave and the work being done. He'd get this dreamy look in his glazed bloodshot eyes. The last checks from the forest service came before winter set in and we faced a four month lay-off. I gave Paco six hundred of my money and said we were even. "I still theenk you rip me off."

I looked at my calloused hands, his stone wall fireplace

with Mexican marble hearth, the perfectly chiseled window, and arch. Gathering my tools, I could see Ramona's sadness. I said, "Paco, I'm sorry I lost your stuff, but you got the better end of this bargain." Just as I pulled out of their driveway, I saw the leader of the gang that robbed me.

The sun glistened off that unforgettable eye, he had the case they'd taken from me under his arm. I waited a few hours and called Ramona, to ask about the situation. When she heard my description of the leader, she said it was Paco's first cousin and I had been scammed. I asked her if she wanted to leave Paco and head south for a warmer climate. She agreed at once.

We've been in Guaymas on the Sea of Cortez for ten years. Ramona brought a king's ransom in jewels. I fish and we garden and grow yerba buena. Our rabbits take lessons from us.

FOUR BEERS A DAY

Quick told me he had to blow town
and asked if I'd run his remodeling
crew for a few weeks, I agreed

He had three semi-crazy black men
working for him, they worked hard
in the dangerous neighborhoods of
north side Milwaukee

Paris was a great painter and drywall
man, but he smoked a bit of weed and
crack and liked skeezer dope whores

Samson was super strong, he did most
of the heavy lifting, he carried steam
radiators alone up and down stairs, he
was six foot eight and three hundred lbs.

Willie was Gene's brother, he was virtually
useless, Gene had fallen on his head off
a ladder and scrambled his brains, he wore
adult diapers and drank four beers a day
and always begged for more

Willie would go buy food and run errands
and do a lousy job of sweeping, Quick said
he was on the payroll to help Gene

I found some aluminum crack pipes and
slimy used condoms where Paris was
suppose to be working, Samson called from
jail, he'd smacked a guy upside the head

Gene's sister called and said Willie had drank
Gene's Old Milwaukee, and sold his butt rags
to an old folks' home, I wasn't cut out to baby
sit grown men, I bought a four pack of Colt 45
and chugged them down like fine champagne.

Spanish Harlem

Hot words spewed from
dog stained fire hydrants
in a sweltering Spanish
Harlem July noche

Vatos sat on concrete stoops
comparing nine and ten
millimeter chrome plated
equalizers, pretty mamacitas

Flashed Ladysmith.38's and
legs all the way to heaven,
they all knew a double tap
was a one-way ticket to gone.

THE LAST POEM

Quick went from a big fat
rejection slip as a poet to
an overnight success, he was
compared to Dylan Thomas

Bukowski, Pablo Neruda, Li
Po, Tu Fu, Ginsberg, and Corso,
audiences and publishers asked
him how he memorized all of

His poems, he said he learned
them by heart, Quick knew he
was a fraud, a big phony, and
possibly a plagiarist, he'd wake

Up and the poems would be in
his shoes, at first he thought he'd
written them in his sleep, so he
set up a camera to record his

Somnambulism, he saw the cats
moving around, but he never rose
from his bed, he was baffled, Quick
only had to read the poems once

And they were recorded instantly,
he was mystified and perplexed
to the point of sheer madness, his
two cats were the only things that

Kept him sane, the nervous break-

down hit him with a full hurricane
force panic attack, he was over-
whelmed and plagued, as he was

Put struggling into a straitjacket
and led to an ambulance, his cats
shoved one last poem in his shoe
and this is it.

ELIZABETH

If I could reach
inside my chest
and rip my heart
out and give it
to you I would

Along with all my
worldly possessions
I would do it gladly

Or turn back the
hands of time and
erase all my faults

If you would forgive
me and speak to me
again after ten long
years of silence

My only child
light of my life
I beg you I need
you I beseech you.

700 PEOPLE DANCING SOMEWHERE

Voices from all over
earth come through a little
radio, 35 people dead in
Jerusalem, so far.

Fog rolls in over Scotland,
elections coming in England,
devolution in a fortnight.

Races in Monte Carlo, Sean
Connery front page news.

Building collapses, crashing
onto a wedding in the City of
David, dead being dug out.

51 dead found in graves in Russia.
Oklahoma bomber of 168 dead.
Macedonia minus Alexander battles Albania.

Beirut against Israel.
Japanese lepers apologized to.

What a world, I sit in the
basement and cry in wonder
and ask God why.

THE PANHANDLE

The snaggled picket fence lay strewn,
ancient teeth in the dustbowl scrub
weed yard, brown yellow sepia washed
clothes hang forlornly on a sagging line

Windblown trees are leaning towers clinging
to red caliche clay and surrendering to the
putrid egg yolk sun, a junky upright piano

A lamp shade and a yucca plant are all that's
left from the Oklahoma tornado, like
the Comanche, buffalo, and armadillos.

ELVIS' DRIED TEARS

Smoofy's teachers refused to call him his nickname and weren't too happy about calling him Jesus, so they settled on Smoofy. He ate lots of frijoles, corn and tortillas, which multiplied his ass power greatly. He could fart on demand and learned many tricks with his potent ass.

Ventriloquism was a specialty, he could make a fart come from his teacher at the blackboard which would crack up entire his class. He made cops fart, the priest in church, nuns, and his mom, anybody he took a dislike to. He learned to use the silent but deadly method. Smoofy could squeak like a dying mouse or rabbit, he could make bird calls, sound like a howling coyote.

He filled balloons with fart gas sold them to his friends as stink bombs to go. Every day he learned new tricks and he became quite versatile. The only thing he lacked was girlfriends, but once he mastered his butt that changed.

ELECTRIC SQUIRREL SHARPENER

Smoofy had lots of pals. They all worked on the brick jobs with Jesus' father as laborers and hod carriers. Reefer was his best pal, he smoked lots of weed. Fucking Aye got his name from not talking much other than saying, fucking aye a lot. Right On was a young soul brother that was popsicle cool. Smoofy was soon given a brick trowel and he was slapping bricks and stone into mortar.

He liked working in the open air, so he could practice farting without too much complaint. Jesus Sr. hired three masons from Mexico and at lunch, they'd build a little fire and warm beans and chorizo. Smoofy loved to eat with them, but he'd cut loose with some ungodly farts. The three Chavez brothers told him he should become an exterminator with his ass. They planted the seed of an idea.

DOG SHIT IN A BONG

Reefer used to complain about washing his car all the time, one day he drove up in a patch work velour car. It was an old Plymouth all greens, blues, reds, oranges, and purples with rust peeking through. It looked like someone had puked on it after a Hawaiian luau. He'd gone to a second-hand store and bought up lots of old fake velvet shirts and dresses and glued them all over his car. We were all waiting for the first rain and hail storm to see how his idea panned out. Right On did a funky chicken alligator dance on the hood, Fucking Aye just grinned and said fucking aye. Smoofy laughed through tears until his old man said work time hombres. Fucking Aye mixed a new batch of mortar after Right On did the walk like an Egyptian while cleaning a wheelbarrow.

BUFFALO JONES MARIJUANA

Smoofy and his buddies started scoring Acapulco Gold at a snooker hall near Albuquerque. It was forty dollars per kilo and came up from Mexico in railroad box cars. Smoofy had always used his brain for business. He bought two pinball machines, set them up in his parent's garage and charged all the kids a nickel a game. He bought three electric lawnmowers with long extension cords from Montgomery Ward's and started a lawn service business.

Smoofy bought some pigs and raised them for pork, feeding them for free from expired store produce. He used the pig shit for fertilizer for his fourteen-foot-tall marijuana plants in Tucumcari. Reefer and him harvested the weed and loaded it in the Reefer Mobile and found a place to dry it. One-night Smoofy's parents weren't home, he had a small party. The cops broke down the front door, but only found some beer, Reefer and Right On had swallowed the joint they had rolled.

The cops tore up the house looking for their stash. They took Smoofy to jail, he stunk up their car and jail so bad, they regretted that decision. Jesus Sr. got him out of the pokey, he told the Chief of Police to stay the fuck away from his son. Reefer came over a few days later and they moved twenty kilos of Mexican gold tops and five gunny sacks of home grown from Smoofy's cottonwood tree house.

CHOPSTICKS AND HAND GRENADES

Smoofy got one letter from Vietnam from Right On. It said, he'd made corporal and he'd tell all his men to get down and they'd all stand up and start dancing and get wasted. A month later Right On's mom told him, he'd been killed. Fucking Aye and Reefer went to Mexico. Smoofy got arrested for marijuana and was given a choice of jail or the army, he chose being a soldier for Uncle Sam for three years. That prison up in Santa Fe didn't like white boys, even if they knew a bit of Spanish. They closed the book on Vietnam and Smoofy ended up in Germany, mostly at the same base as Elvis Presley. Lots of good beer, wine, hash, and ladies, when he wasn't blasting his eardrums shooting howitzer cannons in the cold war games, school was in session. Later in life, Smoofy would realize getting an honorable discharge from the army was one of his greatest and most important achievements, even if it was signed by Richard M. Nixon.

POST OFFICE GIG

A regular job kind of sucked shit through a straw in Smoofy's opinion, but he needed some steady legal income to keep the tax man at bay. He got in at the post office, it was as boring as a macramé class. He still had his weed gigs and worked as a roadie and light show man for several bands in the region. Smoofy cut lots of farts and blamed lots of innocent people.

There was this bleach blonde boss with a big ass that wore tight jeans, she was known as Camel Toe. Her pussy sucked those jeans up snug giving her the old camel toe impression. Smoofy worked on a letter machine with a cute little Asian lady that wore short skirts and no panties. He'd fingerfuck her off and on all night long, until Camel Toe caught him in the act. She told him she needed a couch moved at her new apartment after shift and he had to help or she'd report him. Smoofy knew he was in for a major fuckfest.

They got to her apartment and she grabbed his crotch, unzipped him, got down on her knees and started sucking. He shot his load in her eyes and nostrils and stripped her down. He licked her pussy and she started moaning and groaning and bucking like a wild alligator, she was on fire, her tongue came out and eyes were rolling around in her head. She screamed, "Ha, ha, ha, ha, ugh, ugh, ugh, ugh." This annoyed Smoofy so much he flipped her around, sat on her mouth, and kept farting until she passed out.

MEXICAN WALLS

Poems floating down like sweet snowflakes,
marijuana bricks building walls to Mexico, a
nine stone William S. Burroughs break dances
in a bed of dead batteries and bullet rain

Sounds, thoughts, images, and secret Oulipo
dust sprinkled through this magnum opus
of words. Edgar A. Poe and Dylan Thomas arm
wrestle. Pink Floyd and Led Zeppelin play

Scrabble. I thought of when Cheech and
Chong got pulled over, the cop says, "Your
eyes are red, have you been smoking dope?"
Cheech replies, "Your eyes are glazed, have
you been eating doughnuts?"

MIRACLES NEVER CEASE

I was reading this book
about a man in Russia
who wrote stories and poems

The KGB came and knocked
him around but didn't kill
him they sent him

To Siberia and stole his
bag containing six onions
then my doorbell rang

There was my nympho
aunt bringing six onions
and a bottle of vodka.

POOR GOAT

"I'll be in New York City as soon as I can. Where are you staying?" "I met someone else. He's a photographer in Tribeca. My vagina is on exhibit in a museum and it's making me lots of money." "I thought we were getting married? I thought we had a future together? Now you're parading your pussy all over the Big Apple. I guess it is better I see the true you before we ever jumped the broom." Bagre hung up, thinking every dark cloud has a stinky lining. He looked out from the train station and this weird naked man with a Swastika tattooed between his eyes was driving a Volkswagen. He got out of the VW singing Helter Skelter by the Beatles and pulled a goat from the back seat and was trying to fuck it. Bag wanted to shove a grenade up Charles Manson's ass, but he felt sorry for the goat.

THOUSAND YARD STARES

Hungry bears wait for the red sockeye salmon
to leap the waterfalls into their sharp claws

Pedestrians wait for the light to flash stop and go
The audience waits on the matador or bull to fall

Elephants wait on their seventh and last set of teeth
Prisoners and students wait to be set free

Kids wait on Santa to give them a toy

Veterans wait for help with broken hearts
and souls and thousand-yard stares.

SUPERNATURAL

Sorcery and witchery still flourishes
people need protection, salt strewn
around an encampment helps ward
Off demon attacks, corn meal mixed
with gall of an eagle, bear, mountain
lion, or skunk is potent medicine
Witches live along the Rio Grande,
they steal Mexican sheep and cause
death, beware of shape shifters

SUMMER ON A STICK

She had a champagne thirst, but
I had a Mad Dog 20-20 budget,
she had a t-bone steak appetite,
but I had a grilled cheese bankroll

I almost won a trip to the Great
Wall of China, but had a fear of flying,
we were at the State Fair and she tried
to eat all the stuff served on a stick

There was bacon, spaghetti, duck,
sour kraut, salad, macaroni and cheese,
beaver, python, bison, alligator, skunk,
cougar, ostrich, kangaroo, eyeballs of
all of the above, I told her all I wanted

"Was pussy on my stick" she said,
"Cat?" I muttered some curse words
under my breath and she got pissed
The yellow red sun chinned itself on
the gray horizon, she had split in the
night, I glanced in my closet all that
was left was a bag full of right shoes

She'd taken me to the cleaners, I hoped
she had listened and taken to heart, when I
explained the great deception of mirrors,
smoke, and life and how if you were

Ever arrested you should defecate and pee
in their car and they would instantly release
you on your own recognizance.

THE JIG

A few years before he'd put in a native stone hearth and stone corner reflector for a pot belly stove. The beautiful Mexican lady with the sad eyes was grateful. She made the best chicken enchiladas Quick had ever eaten. Her name was Magdalena and she grew garlic and raised goats for the market in Taos. Quick had learned stone work from his father. Magdalena had two nephews from Mexico, helping her on her little farm. She had told Quick that she'd like to rebuild an adobe chicken house and add onto her house. If he was ever in the region and had time to stop. He parked his sun-bleached Ford under a cottonwood tree and made a tent and campfire. Quick and the boys built wooden forms to fill will caliche red clay and hay for the adobe blocks. After a few days the boys were able to make the blocks on their own. Quick took his stone hammer and Rose trowel and started laying the ground work for wall foundations. He dug down into a corner and hit a metallic sound. Prying the object loose, he cleaned it a bit and saw it was a Prince Albert tobacco can. He shook it and it rattled loud. Opening the lid, it was full of gold nuggets. Quick poured some out into his hand and knew it was a fortune. He yelled for Magdalena and the boys. When they arrived all breathless, Quick showed them his find. Magdalena almost fainted, the boys just grinned in awe. He scooped them all back into the can and gave them to Magdalena. The next day they went to the mining office and bank. She bought all three men new cowboy boots and hats and herself a dress. They pit barbequed a goat and danced a jig. Quick finished her addition and left, he had a rodeo in Gallup and a motel to build there.

Quick's gal pal thought she was quite the chef. Always watching cooking shows and reading books and recipes. One day she was over spicing the food as usual. Quick said, "I think you used too much tarragon." Antoinette said, "You wouldn't know tarragon from a rat turd." He thought she did have a valid point, but she still went overboard. "Do you know how to shingle a banana cream pie?" "Well no." "Martha said to slice the banana at an angle and place them on the cream like a roofer would overlap shingles on a house." "She also said humans peel bananas from the stem end, while monkeys peel from the opposite end, which is much easier." Quick had lots of smart-ass replies, but he kept his pie hole shut. One Thanksgiving he had to work, while Antoinette prepared the bird. When he got home the house was filled with black smoke, she had cayenne pepper, thyme, nutmeg, chives, cornbread, celery, chopped liver all over the cabinets, on the floor, even some on the walls. The stove was burnt all to hell. The turkey was just a small pile of black gray bones. Antoinette's mother and father had just arrived. Quick took them all to Taco Bell. They agreed to try again in two weeks. Antoinette had her French cook book from Mapie, the Countess de Toulouse-Lautrec, wife of the famous painter. Quick went bowling, when he returned, their house smelled terrible. Her parents were there, she had spices everywhere. The meat was dripping green gravy and blood. Quick thought he might save it by putting it on the grill outside. When he got a close-up whiff, he almost fainted. Quick asked Antoinette what kind of meat it was. She said, "Horse." He whinnied and started galloping around the house and right out the front door.

WATER

The old man approached eighty years with no trepidation. The shadows crept closer challenging the sun. Death was a black widow slinking across its web. Getting into an ancient whaling boat, he pointed the prow west. The oars fit his hands like a woman. As land disappeared, icebergs with seals catching fish and polar bears catching seals floated by. He paid no attention, concentrating on the foggy horizon.

The farther the watery path took him the stronger he felt. Gnawing on dried blubber, he tossed chunks to passing seagulls. The sun and wind furrows that plowed his face and surrounded his eyes vanished. His vision became clear and strong. Muscles in his arms, legs, and back bulged with an energy almost forgotten. Where land had once bridged a massive migration only the sea existed. Fifty-seven miles across the Bering Sea passed in the blink of an eye.

Years dropped from the man like layers of skin on an onion. As he reached the tundra laden shore, his language had been left behind with his old body. A young man leaped from the boat. A red wine strength throbbed throughout him. His journey beckoned him south and west. For many miles he saw nothing. Then he noticed the tracks of wolves, he was no longer alone and yet he felt no fear. Cracking ice from a pond he drank deeply. That night sleeping under a billion diamonds, he knew it would be his last as a man. The wolves' content on an easy breakfast bounded down onto the man. His transformation into a caribou took less than a second. Striking out with sharp hooves, it sent several wolves tumbling and howling in pain. The caribou floated up from the ground and flew faster than lightning. It looked down at villages and rivers blurring below.

The snow topped mountains grew up from the earth toward heaven. A cold rain fell into an orange azure turquoise painted stream. A monolithic temple loomed above everything. Monks in saffron colored robes followed each other in solemn order. Workers drove herds of yaks and goats; some carried woven baskets of fish and cackling poultry. Others bore large bundles of wood tied together on their backs. The caribou de-incarnated into a hummingbird and watched the scenes from above. It was tiny enough to escape scrutiny. Flying into an open window in the temple, it followed more steps on its preordained path.

On an exquisitely carved jade pedestal a golden aura emanated. A gaunt parchment skinned monk opened the ruby and emerald encrusted amphora that exuded almost blinding light. It contained three hairs from Buddha. The hummingbird reached its final metamorphosis: a perfect snowflake. It floated down gently from above and settled glistening on the hairs of Buddha and melted

THE TRADE

The pit bull's jaws clamped down on her leg before I knew what happened. The dog had come flying out of nowhere. My daughter was screaming as I clawed at the dog's throat and gouged its eyes. I strained against its neck muscles to no avail. Reaching inside its jaws, I wrenched some relief for my little girl. My fingers were being sawed to the bone.

My wife came running from the house with my big Bowie knife I used for deer hunting. The knife was heavy and razor sharp. I hacked once, twice, sawing the dog's head off. The dog's jaw muscles finally relaxed their grip. My daughter had passed out from the shock. My wife cradled her head as I examined her wound. It didn't look too bad, it was in the fleshy part of her thigh. Then I noticed my hands were bleeding badly. Two fingers were missing from my right hand, the left was minus a pinky. Ripping my shirt up I made bandages for my daughter and myself.

I looked at the dog's head, there hanging out of its mouth were what was left of my fingers. One glassy eye seemed to stare at me in triumph. I gave the head a good kick, I knew I'd made a good bargain. My wife ran after it to retrieve my fingers. A garbage truck came around the corner, squashing the dog's brains all to hell.

SOLDIER

A few stars hung overhead like nail holes in a black wall. Soldier looked up and continued walking at a brisk pace toward the barely discernable tracks. His part in the war was always following warily a few feet behind. He was once an elite shadow of a Long-Range Reconnaissance Patrol.

Chained dogs roamed in the yards of slumbering humanity, growling at the gates of hell. He needed to fight again, to kill to prove himself worthy. Some nights in the waning darkness, Soldier would recall the adrenalin abyss whisper rush, orgasmic sweat soaking his body. Uncontrollable dreams of clean kills and remorselessness stirred an inferno in his loins. Looking around, Soldier saw graveyard emptiness; his heart leaped green mountains of verdure.

It had been over twenty-five years since he last tasted the exhilaration of a human hunt. The evocation of his demons freed and condemned him at the same time. The tracks beckoned him. He carried his cross every time his eyelids closed, every step he took.

Soldier crawled through the underbrush into a distant time. He was miles into Laos, behind enemy lines. Ahead dressed in tan, the uniform of an officer, his target leaned against a thick stand of bamboo, weapon out of reach. Soldier's knife came alive in his fist. He became a dervish of death. Four humans lay staring in carnage at the jungle canopy with lifeless eyes. The stench of blood filled his nostrils, his mouth stretched in an unholy smile. There was no memory of the three men. The woman officer was like a horror movie, he saw his right hand yank her head back, his left draw the blade in an arc across her soft throat. Her head dangled from a flap, death gurgled crimson onto the jungle floor. Her body slumped; her cap askew, long blue-black hair blossomed free like a waterfall at midnight.

Soldier stood over her and studied her face. Even death could not remove or erase her beauty. Dark almond eyes stared at him questioningly, accusingly, his tortured soul screamed, he knelt beside her. In a different world he might have been a young man proposing marriage. He raised her tiny exquisite hands to his lips, tears spilled a turmoil of hate and love. Soldier heard voices.

"Hey mister, have you got a cigarette?" a girl asked.

He looked in the direction of the voice, he was back. Two lovely young ladies were looking at him inquisitively. Soldier offered them two of his smokes. They lit up, their lipstick bright on the filters.

"Some men are after us, can you help us? We need a place to hide."

He looked deep into their eyes. "Follow me. We'll take the side streets." One of them took his hand and rubbed it against her cheek. The other kissed him on the forehead. Soldier felt the taste of blood inside his mouth. He reached inside his jacket for his knife, where it had lain like a scar for too many years.

ON TOP OF OLD SMOKEY

Quickman got his heart broken
by a senorita, so he headed north
determined to join the Mounties

I thought he'd look foolish in a
Smokey the Bear hat, I got a call
from him a few months later

"The Mounties laughed at me, so
I went to a tavern looking for a job,
the bartender asked if I would mind
wearing high heels and licking a few
assholes, starting with hers, I told her
okay if I could rinse them with tequila

One day I was licking this lumberjack's
ass and I looked out the window and I see
two Mounties fucking a reindeer, that's
when I decided to come back home."

VAN GOGH'S SPINACH

Medical marijuana growing became
legal in New Mexico, an amigo homie
was growing some nitroglycerin weed

He was looking for good names and I
came up with Van Gogh's Spinach,
not only because the potency would

Make a potentate beg and cut off both
ears, back in the day I knew a gymnast
with his last name, she was super fine

One night I was hustling nine ball in
the Copper Penny, she seduced me
and led me to my pickup with a camper

She said drive until the corn fields
surround us, we both stripped and the
sex Olympics began, by morning I
felt like a well ridden pommel horse.

THE AVOCADO EXPERT

Three sexy black women were
trying to pick out ripe avocados,
"Excuse me mister, do you know
how to pick the good ones, we
want to make some guacamole?"

I looked at their beautiful full
breasts and said, "You must place
them between your boobies and if
you get horny, they are perfect"

They looked at me like I was loco,
"How could you tell the ripe ones?"
"I'd place them between my balls and if they were good,
I'd get an erection,"

"Why don't you show us?" they said, about that time my
lady arrived with our shopping basket, "Does this smart
ass belong to you?" my lady nodded

"You should keep this crazy motherfucker on a shorter
leash," the nicest one slipped me her phone number and
mouthed call me.

HARMONICA BLUES

His daughter came to
tell him his wife had
died, tears dribbled
off his sunken cheeks

He looked at his harp
and the bars and walls
and tried to smile at
the only good thing
he had ever done

Rubbing the cool metal
through his fingers and
running his tongue over
the holes, he blew

Sad crying hysterical
notes trying to capture
what a woman's body
felt like

What the church bells
and trains sounded like
when he hugged his
family and his daughter
rode his shoulders.

THE MAN THAT SLEPT WITH VERBAL HAND GRENADES UNDER HIS PILLOW

"To fail to take battle to the enemy when your back is to the wall is to perish."
                                    – Sun-Tzu, The Art of War

I was having a creative moment
at the typer when the phone
rang, Caller ID read MOD

Thinking great, a call from the
Mod Squad, Peggy Lipton was
sort of sexy and attractive

A woman's voice said, "Hello
we are not asking for money
this year, but your generosity
in the past has led us to believe
that the March of Dimes can
count on you" I thought bullshit

"We would like you to mail ten
letters to your neighbors on S. 59th
spreading the word of our needs"

I said, "You have me at a bit of a
disadvantage, you know my name,
my address, my phone number and to
me you are only a voice on the phone

You say you work for Jerry Lewis' kids,
but I don't know your name, address,

age, description or marital status

But the bottom line is you want me to
do your job for you by extracting money
in a chain letter, Ponzi scheme from people
near where I live, I'd rather donate money"

"Will you send a check?" she asked

"If you can send me a film of you talking
sexy to me, while you are naked, playing
with yourself, I'll think about contributing"

"You are one sick fuck, aren't you?"

"You have no idea, baby, no idea"

The phone rang again, it was a Democrat.

THE CONFESSION

"Darling, it's our anniversary and I got
you this gift" I handed her a purple
velvet jewelry box
She found a gold wrist chain inside
"I love it, dear" she smiled

"I have a confession to make"
"What's that dear" the smile had vanished
"Well remember when we first got married
and I used to come home real hungry and glassy
eyed and I told you I smoked marijuana"

"Oh heavens, don't tell me you're smoking
that evil substance again"
"No darling, that's not it"
"It's not"

"No, I've decided to become gay"
"You want be gay"
"Yes darling, it's the trendy thing
and I'm just not happy"

"Do you know you'll have to have
sexual relationships with men"
"What in the hell are you talking about,
darling, what language"

"You're the one wanting to be gay"
"No darling, I just want to change my
demeanor and be jolly and cheerful"

She shook her head and gazed at her new
bracelet and then into my dilated pupils.
Helena the Shark

She told me she was Helena
Blavatsky reincarnated, there
was some resemblance, I told
her her breasts reminded me of

Texas, one sort of drooped toward
Dallas, the other curled like a
Texas longhorn in a Waco twister,
her farts were ungodly, I'm talking

Martian strange, I took her on a
short road trip and told her if she
cut the cheese anymore, I'd stake
her ass to an anthill and lather her
with honey, she just smiled, we got
to the beach, I got out our lounge

Chairs and tequila sunrises from the
cooler, I fell asleep when I woke up
a tiger shark was wearing Helena's
sunhat and bloody bikini top and
was sipping an icy Old Milwaukee.

A TORNADO OF TROUBLE

Do you want me?
my luck is lousy, I
live with a landlady
that measures her
tenants booze bottles

Her soul could melt man
hole covers, fire hydrants,
railroad spikes, she gave
me the July blues in winter

A giraffe, lion, magpie in
the cloudless cobalt sky, I
ate a salsa dog taco and had
enough for Cubano tobacco

I get free rent, in a life that's
a joke, while greedy liars and
con artist politicians lead people
down a great path of destruction.

GHOST

When you own
nothing, nothing
owns you, it's
freedom of the poor

He knew long ago
he was finished with
life, only life wasn't
finished with him

He became a ghost
in the mirror, in the
wind, in the shadows
dancing, always dancing.
dancing, always dancing.

PELICAN BOP

"Two degrees in bebop, a PhD in swing, he's a master of
rhythm, a rock 'n' roll king." Lowell George

A buttery sun painted the walls red
her fingers shadowed the tune
ran circles all around the ivories
her bullfrog bass never hitting on the nose
notes traveling high messages in the sky
loop de loop an inverted Jenny bringing it home
when the quiet grew the light faded to black.

SATURN AND JUPITER

Astride a flying llama
seeking yage children with no bones
junkie gringos shooting mezcalito worms
from the heads of beautiful senoritas

The Andes comb the sky
for clouds and thunder
pain dances on the horizon
with Aztec dragons and jade jaguars
Saturn and Jupiter make love to the sun

Frequent coincidence is not happenstance
a force beyond comprehension drives
forgotten rain ghost faces and moon priests
reflect in polished granite
dislocated from the universe

The inhumanity of war strangles
creating perpetual havoc of soldiers
of the magic flag believing
in invincibility and malevolence

Sad bitter eyes look
upon the world stretched
reading nuance of gesture
and futile sound modulation
euphoria snickers behind jealousy
envious emotions and stolen hearts

Greedy fools cripple eternity
and I'm only looking
looking for the way.

GRINGO TACOS

Quick told me about the time he was persuaded to enter a jalapeno eating contest at the New Mexico State Fair. Before he could continue his story, he had an uneven grin on his face and he sort of wiped invisible sweat off his brow. He said he swallowed fifty-one peppers mostly without chewing. Quick said this little Mexican woman that won, ate eighty-seven. She got the trophy, the hundred dollars, and ate one more pepper, just for the hell of it. Quick said, "That night my stomach felt like an earthquake and a volcano were having a fist fight. The next day all those pepper seeds started flowing from me like molten lava." He stuck ice cubes up his ass to no avail. Finally, he spotted a can of Solarcaine in the bathroom closet. He sprayed half a can up his rump. It worked like magic, cooling his butthole down in relief. I told Quick about an adventure I had in Mexico and getting rolled for my wallet. I walked south of Juarez, looking for work. I saw a farm of hot peppers. They were growing, arbol, ancho, guajillo, chipotle, cayenne, and piquin. They gave me a bag to fill and told me I'd be paid twenty pesos a day. I worked until lunch time and they built a little fire and warmed beans, tortillas, and some goat. The food was delicious. After drinking a lot of water, I had to relieve myself. They pointed behind a cottonwood tree. All the workers seemed to be smiling. When I touched myself, it felt like someone had taken a blowtorch to my crotch. I yelled for help. One man came to my aid with a sack of salt and some tortillas. He motioned for me to rub the salt on my afflicted parts. I grabbed a tortilla and started masturbating like a sex crazed lunatic. All the Mexicans were laughing so hard in tears, I started laughing too and before I knew it the heat had stopped.

FIVE FINGER DISCOUNT

Nasty Jack was a greaseball biker
from near the Mexican border, he
got his name from his Levis being
so stiff, he could stand them up in
the corner awaiting his reentrance

He was always working on Indians
and Harley Davidsons, occasionally
he applied his magic to four-wheel ve-
hicles, but he preferred the freedom
of riding in the wind, unless he was

Pulling a big shoplifting job requiring
a crew to cart away the stolen goodies,
his hands were invisible fast, I worked
with him a few times as a distraction
man or driver, Jack knew no fear

I'd entered stores with him and never
seen anything, outside he'd unload
eight huge Porterhouse steaks, three
bottles of Heinz 57 and he'd grab a
rack of fifty packs of Marlboros

Situated right in front of the checker,
he once walked away with two dollies
of booze, one had nine cases of Corona
and the other had top shelf tequila and gin

We never knew what Jack would show
up with next, but he never came home

empty-handed, he wrote a note goodbye and said forget about being thieves, he was going fishing at Boca Chica where the Rio Grande flowed into the Gulf of Mexico.

CRIME IN MILWAUKEE

It's rough all over, for blacks
and whitey in blue and out, a
black man was sitting on a bench in
Milwaukee, whitey popo put 14

Bullets in him, he was supposedly
nuts, he grabbed popo's baton, folks
are walking up and down the streets
waiting for Sharpton and Jesse to speak

And Paula Deen to show up and
cook fried chicken and prove she's
not any more of a racist than any
other God-fearing American

Then we have this 20-year-old
kid that rapes a 101-year-old lady
and wears a dopey grin into court
and he's bragging to the cameras,
saying how famous he is now

A 10-year-old girl on her way
to school was dragged into an
alley and raped by a 26-year-

Old 300 lb. scumbag, he had his
pants down and threatened to
kill the little girl if she ran

Her screams brought people and
the cops arrived, they captured

the animal the next day, but not

Before he molested the girl and
murdered her innocence and purity,
the baby rapist pervert deserves
a slow wretched miserable death.

It Only Hurts When He Cracks a Smile

Quick was hustling nine ball, shooting
with an eagle eye, it was from growing
up on snooker and billiard tables

This dude got pissed off and pulled
out a Saturday Night Special and
shot him right in the ass, his lady
dragged him to the hospital, he felt

Like he was between a dream and a
nightmare, Quick was laying on a gurney
waiting his turn, when they rolled
in a fat heart attack victim, the nurses

Peeled off his shirt, the doc said,
"Son of a bitch, this fucker looks
like a gorilla" they applied the paddles
and turned up the electric juice

His body jumped off the table like a
fish out of water, he was flopping on
the floor next to Quick, they jolted him
again, and his chest hair caught on fire

Lucky for him his lady had marshmallows
and chopsticks in her purse, they were soon
having a nice picnic minus the ants.

VANILLA ZEPPELIN

Combed Yale Park on Route 66
For psychedelics, scored orange sunshine and chocolate
mescaline
I snorted and dropped and smoked
Cannabis clouds floated through the Albuquerque Civic
Center
A surreal hypnotic ambience as red men
Filled pipes with yellow speckled gray peyote
I puffed with them as they turned into coyotes and prairie
dogs
The Fudge hit the fan like a derailed roller coaster
The bass player sawed and rammed his guitar through his
amp
Making people's electrified hair stand on end
The drummer hacked away with his battle axe
At fiery dragons and demonized apparitions
It got funeral pin drop quiet
A blonde lion pranced on stage and screamed
Like ten million rats and cats on fire
Followed by a gypsy with a violin bow and a double neck
guitar
A bevy of beautiful naked women danced in
Then a throbbing pulsating zeppelin hovered above
Raining down rose petals and marijuana buds
The circus became a dervish blur of flying fish and seahorses
I awoke alone and naked in a crater of an extinct volcano
Watching the stars above the Sangre de Cristos
I contemplated next weekend
Hendrix and Iron Butterfly were scheduled.

SCORPION MEZCAL

He ate tortillas dipped in honey
then rode an owl across the
windy Guadalupe Mountains

Possum Sabbath was playing
in a cantina, Quick ordered a
double mezcal with a scorpion
in the bottle ready to strike

The bar keep said, "We don't
carry that poison anymore, it
made my pet coyote go blind"

Quick jerked his hog leg and
laid it on the bar, "Give me
some Zapotec juice from
Monte Alban before I do
something you'll regret"

The band started playing Little
Feat, Quick danced with a pretty
senorita, then they went outside
and jumped into the river of love.

LICKING THE STRIPPER POLE

Maybelle said, "Quickman, you should
start selling wigs door to door, I know
ladies that love fake hair. You could
come to my domino and bid whist hall,
the ladies would eat your white ass with
a fucking spoon. What do you say?"

Quick said, "There ain't no pain with
John Coltrane, baby. I'm no maniac
milquetoast eating mulligatawny soup.
I like to make love and shred time without
injuring eternity and listen to the wind."

They lined up, panthers pacing in stiletto
heels in pools of tears, drinking cocaine in
the kaleidoscope rain. Licking salty limes
and drinking mescal straight from the bottle.

When Quick left three days later, the queen
of cool was on his hook. He had a pocket
full of C-notes. He'd shaved lots of peaches
and licked more than he cared to comment on.

His geisha cowgirl was using a blowtorch on his
triple beam, she had no love or pity in her heart.

PRIORITIES

It was one of those nights,
for a million bucks, I couldn't
come up with a line

"You still want to be a poet?"
Juanita asked, she flipped
four fat slugs into the ashtray

I looked at her & let out a sigh,
"You still don't understand, do
ya honey?" she hiked up her skirt

"Pussy is not what I need"
"What do you need?" she inquired
"A dictionary & a bottle of tequila"

"Fucking faggot" she fired twice
into my typer, blowing it to pieces
she slammed the door as she left,
I went to change my underwear.

FRIDA KAHLO

First time I met my great Uncle Woodrow Wilson Vann he was in the hospital getting his left foot amputated at the ankle because of a diabetes infection. My grandmother, his youngest sister and I traveled to the panhandle of Oklahoma from New Mexico to say goodbye. I was ten years old. I'd heard a lot about Uncle Woodrow, he was a scallywag. He was a self-taught musical genius, playing guitar, violin, mandolin, banjo, accordion, and piano. Woodrow put food on the table playing at dances, fairs, and in churches.

The Vann family was mostly Cherokee and Choctaw. They moved from Tennessee to Oklahoma in a covered wagon. Later they moved south down on the Rio Grande River to Presidio, Texas during Prohibition. Woodrow learned Spanish and would swim across the river and play mariachi and norteno music, and then bring back tequila and mescal. He would tie the liquor bottles up in a sack and put the rope around his neck and swim back north. Uncle Woodrow was on his death bed when we arrived, but was hanging on to life by his fingernails. He wadded and twisted up his sheets into a knot and tried to stuff them into his mouth like chewing tobacco. Woodrow yelled and thrashed about like a captured alligator, scaring me and lots of folks.

My grandmother and I went to Turkey Creek to stay with her oldest sister, Aunt Bertie. Her hillbilly grandsons taught me about using the outhouse and looking out for spiders and snakes, since they had no running water. They took me fishing, taught me how to call a turkey, and how to bark squirrels; shooting a single shot 22 into the tree bark near the squirrel to knock it cold, without damaging the meat for the frying pan. The boys thought I was a real city slicker and took me to the barbershop to get a haircut from a blind barber. I looked like I was ready to enlist in the army; they thought that was real funny.

A few days later we went back to visit Uncle Woodrow and they had amputated his right leg at the hip. He died soon after that and we stayed for the funeral. When the funeral home went to collect Woodrow's body, it had disappeared. No one had an explanation. It's been fifty years since I've thought about this because I came across some old black and white photos of him wearing his sombrero and the post cabin the Vann's had built down in Texas. The cedar posts were driven deep vertical rather than horizontal with viga posts laid atop for the roof beams. I plan on scanning and including photos of this true story.

Sometimes I think the ghost of Uncle Woodrow sort of took up residence in my soul. I've always loved everything Mexican, I learned Spanish, went to Mexico every chance I got, and have been married to a Mexican beauty for thirty years. My lady and I travel often to Guadalajara, the second biggest city in Mexico. Her family moved there from Mexico City when she was thirteen, she was the youngest of eight children. Her father was an accountant, a land owner, and a liquor store inspector in Mexico City. After they moved her mother started a restaurant called The Bonanza, in Guadalajara, it was frequented by firemen and policemen.

We went to Mexico City often to visit her many relatives that lived there. Her Tio Francisco was a captain in the Mexican police force and ended up in the Mexican equivalent to the F.B.I. He studied under J. Edgar Hoover and once caught a famous French jewel thief. Due to his high government position we were able to visit Los Pinos (The Pines) which is Mexico's White House and see many government buildings that are off limits to the public. We saw huge murals done by Diego Rivera, where he met Frida Kahlo. He supposedly was high upon some scaffolding, painting and he told some girls to go get him cerveza and tequila and they refused. Frida was among them; Diego took out his pistol and fired at them like they were cucarachas.

Magdalena Carmen Frieda Kahlo y Calderon born: July 6th, 1907 died July 13th, 1954. She had polio at age 6, making one leg thinner than the other. On Sept 17th, 1925 she was on a bus that hit a trolley car, an iron handrail pierced her abdomen and uterus. She received a broken spinal column, collar bone, ribs, and pelvis. She became pregnant three times, but was never able to have children. Frida met Diego in 1927 and they married in 1929.

I became enraptured by Frida Kahlo, her sad interesting life and her beautiful curious paintings. One of the things that magnetically and magically drew me to her was her having her leg amputated due to gangrene not long before she died. I always thought about her and Uncle Woodrow having the same infirmity. We would visit La Casa Azul, the Blue House that she shared with Diego, Her father built the house. Leon Trotsky and his wife lived there for a while to escape, Joseph Stalin. Frida had an affair with Trotsky and he moved nearby to a fortress like house and was assassinated three years later in 1940. Both of their houses were turned into museums. Diego died three years after Frida and left their house to the government.

In 1938, Andre Breton called Frida, "a ribbon around a bomb." Frida and Diego got divorced in 1939, after she discovered Diego was having an affair with her younger sister, Christina. They remarried in 1940. Frida was a bisexual; she had affairs with Josephine Baker and Isamu Noguchi. Her painting, The Suicide of Dorothy Hale from 1939, always affected me, I'd seen a lady fall from a tall building and splatter on a sidewalk, and it was almost identical to what she captured on her canvas and bloody frame.

After several visits to The Frida Museum we got to know the Coyoacan neighborhood of Mexico City. There were many ceramic tile and pottery shops filled with ornate tile and pottery of all kinds. The Tolstoy Museum was within walking distance of La Casa Azul. It was a surreal wonderful adventure to explore the entire area.

My lady's other Uncle was a foreman in a bullet factory and lived next to a huge bullfighting arena. Tio Luis had a daughter named Juanita. She was a soap opera star and drop dead gorgeous. Her breathtaking beauty stopped traffic, men and women's heads swiveled. She looked like a cross between Liz Taylor and Sophia Loren. Juanita invited us to the nearby volcano mountains, Iztaccihuatl, Mujer Dormida or the sleeping woman and to Popocatepetl, the brave warrior. The mountains resembled what the Nahuatl people had named them for. After the panoramic views and hairpin turn roads in the mountains, Juanita suggested we have dinner at Xochimilco, the Venice of Mexico City complete with gondolas covered in flowers.

Between the canals were many islands with adobe and thatch houses. Joyful people, with chickens, pigs, dogs, cats, turkeys, even horses, and cows lived there. I saw hammocks strung between trees and heard music and singing. It was a happy place, a place of love. My lady and her cousin were in one end of the gondola and I was in the other end with the boatman. Some turkeys were at the edge of water drinking. I let loose with a turkey call I'd learned long ago. The turkeys answered excitedly, lots of them started gobbling. People from the island and boats wanted to see what all the commotion was about. I almost had a turkey riot on my hands, the boatman was laughing so hard he almost fell in the water.

A tall man came out of the shadows and said, "I think you learned that call in Turkey Creek." He winked at me and hugged his woman close. I looked and it was my Uncle Woodrow Wilson with Frida Kahlo, they were alive, smiling, and had two good legs.

SOLDIER BLUES

In the army it was all hurry up and wait

Wait ten meters apart from the next soldier
in the chow line or for the latrine so your
enemy would have a harder target to kill

Waiting for ammo for your weapon
for mail call
for your measly paycheck
on a three-day pass

Waiting for your monthly cigarette and liquor rations
in formation to be inspected like livestock
for the guard duty list to be posted
for stripes

Waiting to call home and hoping your lover hasn't
taken up with your best friend

Waiting for your nightmares of death to subside

Waiting for reentry back to the world
praying for a job and not having to live under a bridge.

GONE AMAZON

He tried normalcy, but love was
a delicate butterfly, in a tornado,
a facade of yearn and desire

Drink helped to forget to remember,
like ships inside bottles evading
the tedium of a burning world

Inside the circular glass walls knowledge
and serenity lived, oblivious freedom
floating on a precipice of madness

One quiet night he finished a bottle
and had a vision of a ship inside filled
with beautiful Amazon ladies, he
swallowed himself and disappeared.

THE LEMON

I was very young when she ordered me to touch her anus. Until then sex was blind wet dreams and masturbation. She liked to turn on the light and throw off the blankets. She was the first to show me her snatch without shame. "Look close, don't be afraid it doesn't bite," she said and pissed in my face. Her small pussy lay hidden like a ripe lemon in her untrimmed black pubic hair nest. "Here," she rolled over and spread her ass cheeks like they were a divine watermelon of delight. I learned to see, to touch, and to ask "like this" until her asshole became relaxed and unashamed, it opened wide and infinite like a smiling baby bird's mouth.

THIRD WORLD COUNTRY

This term has always irritated me,
WHO has the right to classify countries?
I've been married to a lady from
Mexico for over thirty years and lived
overseas for three years in the army, I've
seen poor people up close and personal
In America I've seen hungry children at
soup kitchens in Milwaukee and Chicago,
I've seen my brother veterans living under
freeways and in cold dirty environments
In New Mexico, I've seen hungry frozen
Navajo and Pueblo Native Americans, I've
seen children begging, cold, and shivering
in the mountains and snowy country
In Mexico I've seen children hustling and
working, but never hungry, let me ask again,
is America more concerned with money than
humanity, are we really a first world country?

OCEANS OF PURPLE

The old neighborhood was nearly unrecognizable. Acapulco de Juarez was the happening place from the 50's to the 70's for many of the Hollywood movie stars. Quick found himself fishing the beaches of Guerrero and ending up looking for a job in Acapulco. His Spanish was flawless and his skin so darkened by the sun, he was taken for a Mexican.

In the mercado he saw three well-dressed Chinese men, he asked them for work. They said they worked for the Duke and he might be looking for help. Quick went along with them to a huge mansion. Number One Chinaman was the boss over eight other Chinamen. He asked Quick if he spoke any languages besides Spanish, Quick said no. After testing his ability to drive. Quick advanced in trust quickly and cared for the Duke's horses better than the Chinamen. He was soon made the official driver and was found most reliable.

When Quick wasn't with the horses or polishing the 1955 maroon Rolls-Royce Silver Cloud, he explored Acapulco. Diego Rivera had painted many murals there. Frank Sinatra had a hotel, Errol Flynn, Gary Cooper, and Red Skelton had mansions there. JFK and Jackie took their honeymoon there. The Duke lived in a hotel at first with a long bed, then Johnny Weissmuller took over his room. Number Two gave Quick instructions to go to the airport and pick up an important guest for the Duke.

He waited with a sign for the American black man. Quick loaded his three heavy suitcases into the baggage compartment of the car. The black man asked, "You don't know who I am?" Quick just kept an even look on his face. "Float like a butterfly....does that ring a bell? Do you speakee de English you dumbass taco bender?" Quick just smiled and pulled away from the curb. He thought the Champ was a chump. When they got to the Duke's he wrestled the three bags up to the Champ's room. The Champ gave him a whole dollar.

That night as the Champ and the Duke got ready to feast, the Nine had been hard at work preparing the food. Quick prepared a potion of dried cockroaches and rat manure all crumbled into a fine powder. He asked Number Six which bowl of soup was for the Champ. He stirred in the powder. The Chinamen asked, "What would the potion do? What will happen?" "He will dream he is a cockroach being eaten by a giant rat." "How long will these nightmares plague him?" "It depends on how evil he is and if his heart ever becomes good, maybe forever."

Quick went to the docks where he'd met a beautiful lady, named Liz. Her eyes were bottomless oceans of purple. There was a Van Gogh painting in the main cabin. They cast off and sped north toward the land of the gringos.

THE FORTUNE COOKIE

Your weakness is your strength,
the meaning of existence is none,
love is indescribable so is hate

Autumn leaves are dry potato chips,
grape vines are black and red licorice,
tree branches reach like starving children

When you see the sun, dance it will rain,
you can never love more than one person,
take small steps and drink lots of sake.

THE MARGARITA MACHINE

Quick moved in with a
beautiful woman, she
screamed and bitched
about the movers losing
her margarita machine
A week later when she
found it, she swore the
movers had broken in
and returned it, Quick
Loved her crazy ass, but
got no peace to write, one
night while working on a
poem, she read what he had
(Burroughs cut off his left
pinky at 25, Hitler lost a
testicle in WW1 and farted
so much he got his ass
kicked by his own side)
That sucks she said, that's
not like any birthday card
I've received, Quick packed
his duffel bag and split.

FELONY LITTERING

One night he came back for
his bowling ball, at Margarita
Mama's, he finished a burger,
fries, and a milk shake
The burger bag fell onto her
lawn, she kept Quick waiting
on his ball until, the cops she
called arrived, she insisted he
Be arrested for felony littering,
Quick said the bag wasn't his,
one of the cops offered to throw
away the bag, but she wanted
It to be checked for Quick's DNA,
they refused, she tore the bag
out of the cop's hand and started
looking for a receipt, she
Slammed the front door on all three
men, then jumped in her car and
raced to three nearby hamburger joints
she wanted the workers to pick out
Quick's photo from her cell phone
as a customer or to examine their
security tapes, when the management
refused she started screaming bloody
murder, they called the police
Unlucky for her the same two
cops arrived, they decided her
bullshit had gone on long enough,
they gave her an electricity cocktail.

FASTER THAN SOUND

Quick's lady friend Debra Pickleliquor
enjoyed a glass of whiskey or port, so
he went to buy her some ignorant oil
and milk for his cat and hamburger
He had onions, garlic, and rye bread,
when he exited the store it sounded like
a plane was diving from the sky, then
it felt like Thor's hammer hitting earth
Quick turned the corner and saw the
flying machine in flames jutting out the
window of his flop house, he'd miss Ms.
Pickleliquor, her name suited her well
Jimi, Quick's best friend a black cat
was singed but survived, he poured
milk for Jimi and drank some vino,
they slept until the rain came down.

Sitting Bull Wept

I thought of Sitting Bull
questioning God's abandonment
the winds betrayal

A red island surrounded
by white quicksand
swallowed bit by bit

Each blade of grass
mountain, flower, buffalo,
tears of stone dripped
legends wept smoke.

MY PURPLE HEART BLEEDS FOR AMERICA

Stealing in the name of the Lord,
the country wants soldiers, but
turns a blind eye when they need
help to survive reentry into the world

PTSD is not new it was called shell
shock, bipolar, phobias and panic attacks
are old, they were called nervous break-
downs and mostly treated with booze

That's why you see so many Veterans
living under bridges, homeless, unable
to get or hold a job, they are skilled
killers, nothing more nothing less

America, you've ruined much of your
youth and taken their pride, now they
will have to rely on drugs to stay civilized
and maybe you will be safe, let's pray.

THE GRAPE CIGAR

Mary ripped off the bandage, his brain
tumor was visible, the treatments had
made him worse, she made a blunt

From a grape cigar and some red bud
Columbian, Quick's mouth watered in
anticipation, he told her to put on Tom

Petty singing about dancing the last time
with Mary Jane, he toked hard on the herb
he dreamed of the Louvre and Whistler's

Mother getting out of her rocking chair
and walking like an Egyptian, the Thinker
bumping fists with him and La Gioconda
shedding blue purple crocodile tears.

EL MILAGRO

During the depression my grandfather
wrestled when weather didn't cooperate
to make a good harvest, he was a big strong
man and feared nothing but his family
going hungry or without necessities

The WPA came along and put farmers
to work building roads and bridges, my
grandfather moved to New Mexico and
started a bricklaying company

On Fridays we'd go pay the laborers
and go to the wrestling matches at a
huge Quonset hut with bleachers up to
the rounded ceiling, it was crowded

It smelled of sweat and excitement,
drunks staggered around selling green
tomatoes to throw at the wrestlers you
didn't like, it was a wild adventure I
shared with my grandfather.

Most of the good men were from Texas
and Mexico, the great Lou Thesz with ears
the size of tortillas because of all the head
locks he'd been in, the three Funks

From Borger, Texas noted for their spinning
toe hold submission move, my favorite was
Ricky Romero, he would dance into the ring
and throw tiny sombreros to the crowd

He'd put a choke sleeper hold on his opponent and they would be out and flopping around like a fish, then he'd cover them with a Mexican blanket and bring them back to life.

THE FIRST CAR I WRECKED

My dad went and bought a new baby
blue Ford Galaxie 500, it had a V-8 and
a three-speed standard transmission
shifter on the column, he was proud

He would let me play like I was driving,
I would steer, play shift and honk the horn,
one day I discovered the cigarette lighter

I pushed it in and pulled it out and it
was cherry red hot, I thought I wish
I was old enough to smoke, looking
around for something to burn

I noticed the blue plastic shifter knob,
I got the lighter glowing and stuck it to
the plastic, it melted and filled the car
with a stench, I got my ass beat hard.

RACE RELATIONS

Quick, Armando, and Kwang were
big strong men, they worked in the
Milwaukee valley tannery throwing
cow hides all day long, when they

Weren't building work muscles, they
were guzzling beer and shooting pool,
sometimes men with gym muscles
would try to work in the tannery

They would usually quit before noon,
Quick heard there was big money
pool games at Curly's Tap, it was in

A rough black neighborhood, but
they knew no fear, the place got quiet
when they walked in, Kwang put
two quarters in the pool table

Armando racked the balls, a thin black
man saunters over to the table and mean
eyes the three guys, he said, "What
in the fucking hell are you doing here?"

He pulled out a Glock 9mm parabellum
and chambered a round, "We're just
here to shoot pool, not cause trouble"
"Get your white asses out of here"

Kwang said, "I'm a yellow Samoan-
Japanese" Armando said, "I'm a proud

brown Mexican" Quick looked at the
pistol like a mongoose does a cobra

The black man said, "If you aren't black,
you are white, there is nothing else, now
motherfuckers, don't let the door hit
you in the ass on your way the fuck out."

EL DIABLO

Fifty miles west of Bloomington lies Hillsboro, a monument to middle-class malaise. My guitar playing in Chicago failed to impress anyone, so I ended working for a plumber in the Land of Lincoln. I had enough money for a hot and a cot, my car was burnt toast and axe was soon headed to the pawn shop.

Uncle Bob called from just north of Detroit, Michigan where he was stationed in the Air Force. He said he needed my help for three weeks, packing up his furniture and cleaning his house. He was getting a new assignment in Lubbock, Texas. I told him to mail me a bus ticket and I'd help drive his Chevy Impala to Buddy Holly country for him.

The Air Force base had a huge lake; my uncle said I could fish if I wanted. I went down to docks and there were motor boats and fishing gear for rent. The man that ran the office thought he was big stuff. I had long hair, I guess he thought that made me some kind of sissy boy. There was another young guy there watching how I handled this man. I laid some cash on the counter and told him to fix me up. The other guy asked if he could join me and I agreed. I noticed his eyes seemed strange like a cross between a goat and a Siamese cat. The motor cranked right up, we had poles, and bait and a small ice chest with sodas, sandwiches and chips.

David told me his name and said he was twenty-one and his dad was an officer. He asked if I got high, I pulled out a joint and fired it up. He pulled out some orange barrel tablets and said it was Sunshine. I ate one and we started pulling in sheepshead fish and perch. We started throwing bread crumbs to the circling seagulls. Before we knew it, it looked like The Birds from Alfred Hitchcock. I cranked up the boat and hauled ass for the bait shop. We jumped out of the boat and took off running. The manager started yelling at us for not cleaning out the boat. We were so freaked out, nothing could've stopped us from running. I started hanging out with David, we'd get stoned and drunk. My uncle was none too pleased with this friendship. He told me this kid was bad news and nothing but trouble. He noticed his eyes and said he looked like the devil.

We decided to give fishing another try. The manager told us the boats were off limits to us. David had some sugar cube LSD-25. He told me he was going to dose the dude's coffee. I pleaded with him not to, it was just too cold blooded. The man could flip out and never come back. David dropped two hits on the man. I heard the ambulance sirens and took off. I told David to stay the hell away from me.

Luckily, I was going back to New Mexico a few days later. My uncle said good riddance to David. On the trip southwest, we talked about Kafka, Nietzsche, Heidegger, Kant, Karl Jaspers, the Bible, and Carlos Castaneda and The Teachings of Don Juan. Then we got into great guitar players, I told him I loved Jimi Hendrix, but he'd just died. I also liked Jimmy Page, Frank Zappa, Eric Clapton, and B.B. King. He liked Django Reinhart and Chet Atkins.

MARY JANE

First time a New Yorker moved to my hometown of Clovis, New Mexico and enrolled in my bricklaying class, I helped him and his lady find a place. It was a small trailer house on the edge of town. I noticed something peeking through the kitchen window and went outside, there was a monster marijuana plant duct taped over the roof of the trailer. It took two of us to pull it up by the roots. We chopped it into smaller pieces and hung it to dry. Jose the dude from the Big Apple was impressed, he pulled out a bag of primo smoke and we did some bongs and went and bought a case of Coors. I pulled out a bag of salted in the shell peanuts, he looked at me like I had leprosy and he explained about his allergy to them. I told him peanuts grow all around Clovis. Jose said it would be like being bit by a rattlesnake for him to eat one. I thought it must be a bit of an exaggeration. That night I made it home and dreamed about aliens, but instead of landing in Roswell, they landed in a peanut field. The aliens made Jose gorge on goobers, his body started inflating like a blimp and soon he was floating away over the horizon. I woke up and I was in bed with his woman. She didn't appear happy.

Booze Death Poem

Sitting on an Umbrian mountain top
missing my lady, I decided I'd drink
myself to death, I'd been sober for ages

Fresh beverages with grapes and strawberries
absinthe with cayenne salt and chile infused
mezcal, brandy sidecars, tincture of amaro in
a Manhattan burnt spice julep, artichoke Cynar
king of carrot flowers, coconut oil and Thai
basil laced with gin and vodka, rum and
scotch with ginger, lemon, and egg white

The sky purpled, the wind gathered thunder
the storm sagged toward the ground, funnel
clouds wobbled down vacuuming everything
in their path, relentless unstoppable

Suddenly I'm holding a list, it appears to come
from a doctor or a hospital, laughing I read it:

678 cases of diarrhea;
167, constipation;
26, hemorrhoids;
456, indigestion;
372, foreign bodies in the eyes;
375, severe headaches;
648, episodes of fainting and exhaustion;
71, cases of extreme flatulence;
178, cases of teeth that hurt like hell.

Rock of the Agony

In the Garden of Gethsemane
eating Spanish onions dipped
in salt, bound for Bethlehem

Under the Jerusalem olive trees
drinking dirty martinis made with
Russian vodka tasting Beluga caviar

No buckets of money or nose candy
cocaine while licking golden honey,
only memories of enchiladas, paella,

Baked Alaska, brimstone eight balls
in a Texas tornado near the Alamo,
and dancing the Cotton-Eyed Joe

I'm headed to the Pawn Shop of Love
baby, because I'd rather be lonesome
than have your damn foot on my neck.

SEAGULL BOOGIE

For a week I'd been watching
a seagull in the parking lot,
it was mostly white with gray
feathers near its tail, an orange
beak and marble black eyes

It would fly down on its four
foot wing span and perch on cars,
waiting for someone to discard
part of their lunch, so it could
feast on scraps, forever watching
for a meal and a place to defecate

Warm weather arrived, I lowered
my windows to head home after
a long hard day, the cannibal bird
flew in the passenger side and started
a ferocious pecking frenzy on my face

Knocking my lit pipe from my lips,
sending a glowing ember onto my
testicles, I tried to keep my car from
crashing and looked in the mirror

A cop car with cherry lights flashing
was right behind me, I managed to
stop, opened the door and fell into
the street, the men ran toward me
with pistols in hand, the seagull flew

From my car, snatched a hat from one of

the cops, then flew toward the Milwaukee
River, noticing the men in blue staring
at the departing bird, one had a piss
stain down his left leg, I just smiled
and tried not to laugh.

NEPTUNE

Shrieking tumbling notes
blended with NYC rain,
trains colliding in the
Valleys of Neptune

Hendrix rebounded and
echoed off ships, passing
through bleeding heart fire

Putting a fin in the open
guitar case, I opened my
chapbook, the musician
nodded as I read and watched
the magic Machine Gun

His invisible fingers kept
playing as the ivory Fender
went behind his back and
came out in flames

Blinded by lightning, I
looked up and all that remained
was a bluebird feather
and a guitar pick.

EIGHT RULES FOR DEFECATING IN NATURE

1. Never wipe with a pine cone, porcupine,
poison ivy, or prickly pear (the 4-P's)

2. Never lower your laundry near a bear or
mountain lion with an erection, a diving eagle,
a flock of turkeys or Canadian geese

3. Never drop a load in a snake, badger,
coyote, woodchuck, or prairie dog hole

4. If a skunk or rattler happens by while
you're in the act, don't try to compete,
compare, or make friends

5. Beware of hillbillies with banjos, men
in prison garb, and women with facial hair
and bulging crotches

6. Always use insect repellent liberally

7. Sand rubbed gently in your crack and
rinsed will remove undesirable crustiness,
check sand for fire ants first

8. Cover your scat.

Catfish McDaris' most infamous chapbook is "Prying" with Jack
Micheline and Charles Bukowski. His best readings were in Paris at
the Shakespeare and Co. Bookstore and with Jimmy "the Ghost of
Hendrix" Spencer in NYC on 42nd St. He's done over 25 chaps in
the last 25 years. He's been in the New York Quarterly, Slipstream,
Pearl, Main St. Rag, Café Review, Chiron Review, Zen Tattoo,
Wormwood Review, Great Weather For Media, Silver Birch Press,
and Graffiti and been nominated for 15 Pushcarts, Best of Net in
2010, 2013, and 2014, he won the Uprising Award in 1999, and
won the Flash Fiction Contest judged by the U.S. Poet Laureate
in 2009. He was in the Louisiana Review, George Mason Univ.
Press, and New Coin from Rhodes Univ. in South Africa. He's
recently been translated into Spanish, French, Polish, Swedish,
Arabic, Bengali, Mandarin, Yoruba, Tagalog, and Esperanto. His
25 years of published material is in the Special Archives Collection
at Marquette Univ. in Milwaukee, Wisconsin.

CPSIA information can be obtained
at www.ICGtesting.com
Printed in the USA
BVHW031028211218
536174BV00002B/146/P